For everyone who has felt objectified or felt like they have lost agency over their own body. Even for a second.

To my parents Margie and Roy, who taught me about love, feminism and that centring my life on my passions is the only way to live. My sister Stevie for her inexhaustible sense of humour and for being the most incredible example of resilience. My partner Jordy for being what can only be described as my equal in every way, my best friend and silent support system through the whole campaign, and finally to Ryan Whelan – The Hammer – my lawyer and friend, for being a brilliant male ally, a patient and kind teacher and for considering running for Prime Minister in the future.

#WeForWhelan

BE THE
C?E

DATE DUE

			PRINTED IN U.S.A.

WITHDRAWN

sphere

SPHERE

First published in Great Britain in 2019 by Sphere
This paperback edition published by Sphere in 2020

1 3 5 7 9 10 8 6 4 2

A CIP catalogue record for this book
is available from the British Library.

ISBN 978-0-7515-7789-1

Typeset in New Baskerville by M Rules
Printed and bound in Great Britain by
Clays Ltd, Elcograf S.p.A.

Papers used by Sphere are from well-managed forests
and other responsible sources.

Sphere
An imprint of
Little, Brown Book Group
Carmelite House
50 Victoria Embankment
London EC4Y 0DZ

An Hachette UK Company
www.hachette.co.uk

www.littlebrown.co.uk

CONTENTS

SECTION TWO: CAMPAIGNING

INTRODUCTION TO THE NEW EDITION

A couple of months before The Voyeurism Act came into force, I had to come to terms with the fact that my original plan – to tirelessly campaign for two years, change the law and then go back to work – wasn't going to happen. This was where the work began. I was preparing to leave my full-time job in advertising – and more worryingly, I was also planning to tell my bosses I would not be working my notice, because to do so would have meant rejecting all press, speaking and media opportunities to educate around the upskirting law. The goal posts had continuously shifted. It's funny that, isn't it? First, I thought the work began with learning about gender inequality, after I'd been upskirted at a music festival in Hyde Park in 2017. Then, I thought the work started when I launched the campaign to make upskirting a sexual offence – but then I thought it really began when I launched the legal case with my lawyer, Ryan. However, when the law was passed in April 2019, I realised that the work never begins if it's made for you. It's always there. It'll cease to exist only when I do.

The law had changed, but had people's minds? Unless you educate as many people as possible on their rights, they don't necessarily know what options they have or how to use them. That became the next job, and this book was part of that. I remember making a coffee, and walking over to my dining room table with the intention of setting myself up and beginning to write my – at that point untitled – debut book. I popped my coffee on the table and suddenly realised I didn't own a laptop. I'd never been able to afford one, and the one I used before was owned by my employer at the creative studio I worked at as a copywriter. I'd just given that laptop back when I left my job to, ironically, write this book. Somehow, the fact that I didn't own a device to write a book hadn't occurred to me. My first thought was: 'I'll write it on my phone and borrow someone else to edit it' (okay, Gina). This gives you an idea of the state of mind I was in around that time. Overwhelmed, but resourceful. The two adjectives that one might use to describe my entire campaign. I was truly in a washing machine. My job was changing; my dreams were changing, I was mid-flight, thrust into the public eye. The last two years of campaigning had shifted my perspective on not only society but, more confusingly, my place in it. It had catapulted me from the white feminist thinking I had been gobbling up in my early twenties to the intersectional lens I needed as a white woman doing this work. The learning curve had been steep, and I had to learn at break-neck, whiplash speed.

My feet hadn't touched the ground, and yet somehow I was ready to write a book.

When my laptop arrived a few days later (one I wouldn't actually own until 2020 when I'd paid it off), I felt a huge pressure to write some weighty political text; a book that would change everyone's minds and make all who read it believe they could change the world. I freaked out. I was so deep in the belly of momentum, pressure, expectation and whatever else the public eye brings into your life, that I felt this crushing expectation to live up to the media's representation of me: a 'changemaker', an 'inspiration', a 'remarkable woman' and 'feminist icon'. But I didn't really want to be those things, because they're bigger than the work. I wanted to be the work, and *with* people – not being held above anyone else. I still do, I'm just more confident saying it now. As soon as I tapped the last few letters on the first page I knew what I actually had to write: the book I needed when I sat in bed thinking 'I want to do something but I have no idea where to start here' four days after I was upskirted in 2017. I needed a book that made me feel capable, not 'too young' or 'too emotional', one that removed the 'you're an amateur' from my head and replaced it with 'you're passionate and unjaded and, most of all, you're *right*!" After that realisation, I wrote this book in two months – not because it was easy to write, but because I was finally able to just pour everything I wish I'd known at the beginning into one place. All the simple-but-you'd-never-think-of-it stuff. I hoped I'd create a book that was completely un-intimidating, totally practical, accessible and, above all, a piece of work that anyone who wanted to 'do something' could use.

Since I released *Be The Change*, I've continued to work in writing, speaking, advocacy, but for the first year after the book published I *needed* a break. The type of campaigning that brought in The Voyeurism Act left little space for anything else. It consumed me and wasn't healthy. When I started educating people about the law, I was doing *a lot* of speaking, events, discussions, panels and talks. Everyone wanted a piece of me. In private, I was educating myself on what gender equality and human rights meant for other people. I didn't want to be someone sitting on panels talking for other women; I wanted to be someone who told their personal experience through an intersectional lens where it was relevant, but pulling out of other panels and recommending other people instead where a different voice was needed.

As 2019 ticked along, my law began to be used. You'd be forgiven for thinking that, as the most visible person responsible for an amendment to the law, I'd be kept abreast of its usage, but you'd be wrong. I found out through the media, like everyone else did. I'd be tagged in stories and scroll past cases on my timeline. I had an idea of what was happening, but to know how well something is working you need comprehensive, comparative data. However, access to this data was *always*, throughout the entire campaign, a struggle for me and it didn't become easier when the law changed. At the beginning of the campaign I was told by lawmakers and police that upskirting 'wasn't a big problem' because there were few cases on it. When officers looked into the recorded offences of each constabulary, it was incredibly hard to identify which was upskirting because it wasn't a specific offence so the language didn't exist. When I worked with the Press Association to attain data on reports of upskirting through a freedom of information request, some constabularies, including the Met police refused to release their figures. Because of this, it's hard for me to give you a full picture of what the law has achieved, but I think the figures we *do* have show a clear upward trend of increased awareness, accountability and understanding of the issue.

I was upskirted in July 2017 and started my campaign at the end of that month. Between April 2015 and April 2017, there were 78 reports to police with 11 resulting in suspects being charged. It's important to note though, that only 15 forces, out of the total 43 in England and Wales, provided data for this period because many simply didn't have it. Upskirting had never been a mainstream conversation before, so when the law changed more people than ever knew it was a chargeable offence. In the first six months after The Voyeurism Act became useable, data from 35 police forces found there had been 153 incidents reported to them in the 182 days since the law was created. That amounts to almost *one report of upskirting to police every single day.* No matter how you look at it, this is a huge increase; from 78 in two years to 153 in six months.*

---

* https://www.met.police.uk/cy-GB/SysSiteAssets/foi-media/
metropolitan-police/disclosure_2019/december_2019/information-rights-
unit-allegations-of-upskirting-reported-to-the-mps-since-april-2019

The downside, though, is that convictions are still notoriously tricky to achieve. Convictions have increased, but not exponentially – although the convictions that have occurred have been important. The law is not retrospective, which means that you cannot be charged and convicted of this act if it occurred prior to the law coming into force in April 2019, but within the first six months we'd prosecuted ten men, two of which were convicted paedophiles. One man of 50 years was the first person jailed, after he was caught stalking teenage girls around a supermarket in Lancashire, and another man of 51 received the strongest sentence after filming under women's skirts (including a 16-year-old girl) through a hole in his bag at another supermarket in Surrey. He was detained after the girl's mother reported him and, horrifically, 250,000 indecent images of children were subsequently found on his devices. He had also previously been convicted of upskirting (under outraging public decency) and told the officers he'd bought a spy pen to continue his voyeurism.

Both these men were jailed for their actions. The second for 28 months – with the upskirting charges accounting for 12 months of that, and the other for two years. As were two more perpetrators in the first year of the law. All these men were added to the sexual offenders list – something that would be impossible without upskirting being a specific sexual offence. You see, this law change does more than just what it says on the tin. Some critics of it claim it 'doesn't do enough to protect women' (hell, professors have even written papers on just that), but I believe they fail to see a critical reality here: this law was never just about catching upskirters. It's specificity doesn't necessarily limit it; it's just another tool to catch sexual predators of all kinds. And it does just that, because as I've found in my work and the Crown Prosecution Service has found too, *upskirting is often a marker of a wider pattern of non-consensual sexual abuse.* Often perpetrators of upskirting have committed other sexual offences, and this act – that often happens in public place – can be where they're caught. As Siobhan Blake, CPS national lead for sexual offence prosecutions, said: "Some of those convicted are dangerous repeat sex offenders, which shows how upskirting is no trivial matter and can indicate a wider pattern of predatory behaviour." All sexual violence is connected, because it signifies a lack of consent and therefore power.

The punishments The Voyeurism Act enforced are proportional to the level of offending and the seriousness of the activity. For instance, a man who takes one photo to humiliate someone – as my assaulters did – will be treated entirely differently to someone who has spent years collecting thousands of non-consensual upskirt videos and photos. Although all versions of upskirting are unacceptable, humiliating, painful, and should be taken seriously, using a range of punishments means that we aren't just jailing all people who upskirt, as the newspapers would have you believe. When the media started to pick up on the law change, the headlines were usually something like: "NEW UPSKIRTING LAW TO JAIL OFFENDERS FOR UP TO TWO YEARS", which positioned The Voyeurism

Act as an unforgiving, political tool to push incarceration. Although I could control what I gave to the media (to a point ... when a story gets big, it takes off without you) I couldn't control their angles. I hated that that my proud face would be printed next to these kinds of headlines, because, personally, there are parts of the prison system in the UK that I hugely struggle with. I believe we could have a more effective, humane and rehabilitative prison system, and I also know that Black and non-white people are grossly overrepresented in UK prisons. Analysis for the Lammy review found that the odds of receiving a custodial sentence are significant for non-white people with Black people (53%) Asian (55%), and other ethnic groups (81%) more likely to be sent to prison for an indictable offence at the Crown Court, even when factoring in higher not-guilty plea rates.* So, the idea that the imprisonment part of the law was being focused on heavily was uncomfortable.

To prosecute someone for upskirting, you need to have significant evidence and in reality upskirting is, much of the time, a hard offence to prove. The majority of the time it's a non-contact offence (you may not feel anyone touching you or even know its happened), it's routinely concealed by specialist devices, hidden cameras and more, and it can happen in crowded spaces, which means it's really hard to see happening. Eye-witnesses are the most common form of evidence, but in no way guaranteed with each case. Without

---

* http://www.prisonreformtrust.org.uk/WhatWeDo/
Projectsresearch/Race

much evidence it's hard to secure a conviction – like any sexual assault. Because of this and a whole host of societal pressures and biases most people don't even report that they've been upskirted. Put all this together and you have a system where most people who upskirt others are getting away with their actions with absolutely no accountability.

Lack of reporting + lack of evidence = low conviction and prosecution rates.

When people are convicted and/or prosecuted it's because there's enough evidence to prove the offence happened beyond reasonable doubt. No easy feat. For an individual to be jailed for this offence means there needs to be overwhelming evidence of consistent and calculated assault, as was the case with the two case studies above. Those who commit this offence continuously and in public are more likely to be caught and that's reflected in the data. My point is, although we don't have a huge amount of information to go on yet as this loop hole in the Sexual Offences Act has only been closed for couple of years, anecdotal evidence shows incarceration will be for absolute worst case offenders who are considered a serious danger to society. Others will be placed on the sexual offenders register, forced to pay fines and sentenced with community orders too.

I've struggled to become comfortable with the fact that after I changed the law I had to let it go – I couldn't control how it was enforced. One case that particularly haunted me was in 2019, when Daren Timson Hunt, 55, used his phone to film up a female passenger's skirt while travelling on the

London underground. At the time, he was a barrister at the Department of International Trade, where he worked as the head of a European Union legal team. A *barrister* in one of the highest offices in the UK. Daren admitted hiding his phone under his leg to take a sexually gratifying video of a female passenger's crotch while she made her way to a job interview. The woman in question went on the say that the incident has deeply impacted her day-to-day life, that she now can't wear skirts and avoids public transport. I know how she feels. Daren was sentenced to a 24-month community order with a 35-day program requirement, 30 days of rehabilitation activity and 60 hours unpaid work, and was put on the sexual offenders register for five years. When paparazzi got wind that 'the first man had been convicted with the new upskirting law' they descended on him, snapping photos as he tried to enter his workplace. His response? A frustrated 'stop taking picture of me!" How ironic, Daren. That's all she wanted, too. The bit that really enrages me was that a disciplinary tribunal decided *not to ban Daren from his profession*, after accepting his argument that the assault happened in the 'heat of the moment' and because of work pressure. Instead, he was suspended for six months. Don't ever tell me that accusations ruin men's lives. They often don't even ruin careers. The write up of this case consisted of a 'fall from grace' narrative, how stressful his work situation was, how his wife was ill and how many hours he worked a week, as if justifying his choice to assault someone.

This case forced me to really start questioning myself and my work. Did the law work? What was my role now? Do

I fight the outcome of each and every case? I had to settle on no. I don't have the access or the expertise, but I *do* have moral clarity and a platform. I helped to create a law to protect people, and now my job was to educate both the system and the public on that law, support the victims of this assault and make them feel seen, collect data on prosecutions conviction and reports each year, and use my platform draw attention to cases where I don't believe it's being used properly. Maybe one day, I'll see that as 'doing enough'. For me, the core of activism is that you're never done and you've never learnt enough or done enough. But every now and then, for a fleeting moment I am forced to see that I've done something big. Something that has a real impact.

In the two years since I finished *Be The Change*, the world has turned upside down. Events include:

- a deadly pandemic – that made us feel like we're living in a sci-fi movie, and forced the most marginalised and forgotten in our communities to live under an even more oppressive state
- India and its farmers creating the largest protest movement in history
- Britain leaving the EU
- Australia experiencing its worst bushfire year in modern history
- An insurrection of Trump supporters breaking into Capital Hill
- China continuing to imprison Uigher Muslims in genocidal camps

This is by no means an exhaustive list, and more a way to illustrate the period we're living through. I also don't write it to scare you, but to prove that the world is terrifying, huge and difficult to comprehend. This has been the case for generations, and to struggle, be scared and feel overwhelmed by it is to be human. Your feelings are a normal reaction to a modern world which isn't working. I feel the same. I write this to show you there is work to be done. These oppressive forces continue to exist, and so we must work harder.

To make the world a better place, there is one thing you must never let go of: hope. Sure, there will be days when it doesn't show up or you can't feel it, but that's okay. Sadness and fatigue get in the way of hope. I get those moments often; they come with the territory. I had a few days like this when I heard of the Daren Timson Hunt case. You see, even if you do something objectively big, or even if you manage to change something structurally there will still be these moments where something doesn't go as planned. Where another barrier pops up. The barriers will always keep coming. That's the nature of our job, so we have to take time out, lean on people around us then tap back into our community and use each other to keep going. Hope is an enduring part of our existence – like love – but it's not this nebulous mystery. It's something you create. It doesn't come from nowhere; it springs from the people who speak out about their stories, from the person who refuses to shrink in the face of a challenge even though their knees are shaking. It's created in tiny, everyday actions, as well as big, loud ones. Hope is down to us. We *have* to create it for each other, because without hope this work doesn't happen. You have to believe in something better to be able to move towards it. And look! Hope is here too! Since I wrote *Be The Change*, some incredible things have also happened, like:

- The second person in the world is cured of HIV
- Humpback whales recover from near extinction.
- Trump is voted out of office as Democrats win the election and flip the senate, and is impeached (twice).
- Britain goes two whole weeks without coal.
- *Police brutality in America* kicks off the biggest ever global right civil rights movement.
- The supreme court rules that LGBTQ employees are protected by civil rights employment statutes.
- Polio is officially eradicated from the continent of Africa.
- Germany committed to turning 62 military bases into nature reserves.
- Scotland becomes the first country to make period products free.

Every single one of these changes was started by regular people working together, sometimes over years, to push the dial forward. None of this progression came from divine intervention, it was simply people like me and you, working in specific areas applying our skills, levelling up, gathering information, pushing, taking risks, partnering up with others, communicating the problem and fighting to put procedures in place to change it. All of this is to say, you've picked up this book during an important, turbulent moment in history. And now, more than ever, people need to be pushing for progress. People need *hope*. That's why I've worked on different projects since the law changed; I care about so many issues, because they're all interconnected. When the pandemic started I create a petition and online campaign to get Deliveroo to add an option to buy a meal for an NHS workers to their app. They recognised my campaign and added the function. It was a small thing, but it created hope.

In July 2020, I worked on something that felt like I'd come full circle. During the upskirting campaign I learnt a valuable lesson: the transformative nature of people coming together across communities. Ryan went out on a limb for me and decided to represent me pro-bono to amplify my voice and lend his skills to a cause that didn't generally didn't affect him. He kept me front and centre of the work and instead of taking over advocated for me throughout. He got me in the rooms at the table and made them listen to me. He was, what we love to call, an ally. I decided that when this was over, I would pay it forward. I would lend my skills to someone who needed them. So when I saw Instagram was censoring a picture of Nyome Nicholas-Williams by Alexandra Cameron even though it didn't break any community guidelines, I offered my support and my platform. I asked followers to flood Instagram with Nyome's photograph under the hashtag

#IWantToSeeNyome. I sat down and researched censorship of plus-sized Black bodies on the platform. I sat in bed and figured out a roadmap for Nyome to get Instagram's attention, and I identified the person we needed to get in front of – Adam Mosseri. Through talking to Nyome and Alex I figured out where I could put my skills in order to help them get what they needed: accountability. We figured out what we were asking for and what policy we needed to change, and eventually our four months of work resulted in a change to the nudity policy and specifically the breast-squeezing guidelines that were disproportionately affecting plus sized women and, of course, Black women the most; white thin women's bodies are nude all over instagram, and even white plus-sized bodies are removed less. The reality of doing this work though, was this: I as a white thin woman do not know what Nyome is going through, so it's not my campaign. And it's not my place to act as if I 'got it', or take up more space than I needed to in order to help. There is a lot I don't know about in terms of racial bias and fatphobia, however much like to think I self-educate. I will *never get it*. But what I do get is how to plan, how to organise, write, get media coverage, identify advocacy figures, create public pressure and turn it into political momentum. So my job was to do that, behind the scenes, to help her win. Because she deserved to win, and it wasn't about me. You see what I mean about hope? We create it for each other because we are in this together.

All of us care about something, and all of us have skills. All you have to do is be honest about them, figure them out and put them together. It doesn't matter what it is you're fighting for, if it's something you're doing intentionally, for the good of the collective and you're doing it little and often trust me when I say *it is valuable*. I hope you know that reading this book makes you part of a club of people who are creating hope, too. People like Hanna and Ida who changed the law in Germany to make upskirting illegal after being inspired by my campaign. Women like Sol who created Give Your Best, a free online shop for refugee women and women seeking asylum who need clothes and community. They all read this book and used it, and I hope it makes you see that progress is something you can push for too. I hope it reminds you that the other side have already won if they've convinced us we can't achieve change, and that our job is to disprove that. Thank you for picking up the second edition of *Be the Change*, it's really your toolkit for creating hope and a safe place to start. I believe in you.

PROLOGUE

9 July 2017

It was thirty degrees, every blade of grass in London had been burnt to a golden ash, and I was so bloody happy because I was seeing The Killers in Hyde Park with my older sister, Stevie. Stevie is my best friend, and that year we hadn't seen each other all that much. We'd grown up listening to and loving The Killers so we both decided to fork out the £80, which we couldn't afford, to have that one day together in the sun and forget the stress of London life. We'd got ready, dressed up, and were so excited about a day of laughing, dancing and finally seeing our favourite childhood band together. As kids who had grown up with a musician father, and been in and around the music industry, gigs were a happy place. Music was, and still is, escapism for us, and this day was meant to be just that. As we weaved our way through lounging festival-goers, I noticed a guy lying on the grass looking up at the sky. My eyes were drawn to him because he'd planted himself in an unusual spot: he was lying with his head obstructing a strip of grass that people were using to get through the crowds, and was making no effort to move, forcing them to step over him. I got closer and saw his eyes dart to the legs of a girl weaving around him. It was then that I realised he'd deliberately positioned himself so that he could look up the skirts of girls and women rushing towards the main stage. Without thinking, as if it was second nature, I patted down the back of my skirt and hopped past him. I didn't challenge this guy on what he was doing. I didn't call him out. Looking back now, I wish I had, but I suppose, like most women, I was used to it.

An hour later we were standing in the 60,000-strong crowd waiting for the band to take the stage when a group of men started paying me unwanted attention. This was something I'd become accustomed to – I was used to it and I knew how to deal with it. Or at least I thought I did. One of the guys was wearing a Killers T-shirt and a trucker-style cap and I clocked him as the ringleader immediately. Although I made it clear that I wasn't interested, he started persistently hitting on me with a smirk. I rebuffed him firmly, with a smile – as always. Be polite, Gina; don't make a fuss. In truth I was trying not to anger a man who was intimidating me. Men who I don't know that use intimidation to coerce me into what they want – attention, inappropriate conversation or otherwise – make me feel nervous. They always have. I've seen too much and heard too much not to feel that way. So being polite was, and still is, a way to keep myself safe. He tried again, and again, and again, and when he finally realised I wasn't biting he announced, loudly, that he bet I was 'good at giving blow jobs'. His mates laughed. For me, the mood quickly turned; a line had been crossed and Stevie and I bristled. I felt us sort of lock together with an unspoken acknowledgement that this had taken a sharp turn to exactly where we had thought it was going, but hoped it wouldn't. One can of gin and mixer down, I decided to communicate to him that this would end here, and so I said he sounded like a twelve-year-old. Stevie laughed. I turned my back on him once more to show I wasn't interested in any kind of conversation or physical contact.

Minutes later I was aware of them stifling their laughter behind me and an uneasy feeling simmered up in my belly. I instinctively knew that my remark had angered or embarrassed the trucker-hat guy and now I had this unnerving feeling that he had done something to me. I just wasn't sure what. But I knew this kind of guy wasn't one to accept being rejected. I was partially surrounded by the group, as you often are in a festival crowd, and in front of me stood one of the biggest guys – a blond, muscly type. He was on his phone, and around the side of him I happened to catch sight of the screen. He had a chat on WhatsApp open, and a thumbnail of a photo taken up a woman's skirt, that he had been sent, stared back at me. I could see it clearly. It was well taken in broad daylight, and you could see it all: her thighs and buttocks, her pubic hair and her genitals covered only by a thin, slightly twisted strip of underwear. It was a horrible picture and I knew instantly that it was me.

Without thinking, I lunged and snatched the phone out of his hand, raising it up in the air. 'You've got a picture of my vagina? *What is wrong with you!?*' I bellowed, beginning to choke up. He spun round and grabbed me by the shoulders, shaking me and shouting that it was 'a picture of the stage'. He was huge. I slapped him. He screamed something in my face and his grip tightened. As he shook me, I made a point to look directly and systematically into the eyes of the people around us and to say repeatedly 'help'. I heard my sister crying and shouting at the guy, but I could tell she wasn't next to me, so I instinctively passed the phone to a woman I didn't know. The blond guy got in her face demanding she pass it over, but she refused and held it firmly behind her back. To this day I am desperate to find out who she was. What a hero. The next thing I know, two guys in the crowd shouted for me to run and the woman slipped the phone into my hand. I tore off, pushing through the sea of people, begging them to let me past as The Killers took to the stage and the first song blared out. I thought I'd lost him, but as I emerged from the last stragglers of the crowd, I heard his feet pounding the dusty grass behind me.

I came into view of the security staff and saw concern flood their faces. I managed to reach them just before the blond guy did, ducking behind a hefty guard, who brought the guy's momentum to a stop and shielded me as the guy took a swipe at me. Immediately I blurted out what had happened and the guard quietly and calmly told me to slip the phone into his pocket. As I did, Stevie came speeding out of the bouncing crowd and held me while the blond guy spat and shouted that his friend had taken the photos. 'Fine,' the guards replied, 'go get him then.' He wouldn't. We were led over to the police and I remember physically exhaling when I saw a male police officer accompanied by a female officer coming towards me. 'She'll get it,' I thought to myself. 'She'll understand.' They separated me and the blond guy and asked me what had happened. I was crying pretty hard at this point, but I managed to calm myself down enough to get it out in detail. The security guard backed me up and the police were sympathetic. It's still so clear in my mind what the male police officer said to me next. He told me, with genuine dismay, 'You should be able to go to a festival in thirty degrees and not be worried about someone taking a photo up your skirt.' I exhaled. They got it. They were on my side. After we'd talked they headed over to speak to him. As they did, I remember trying to dance to the song The Killers were playing – 'The Man'. I was desperately attempting to pretend everything was okay, but was just limply shuffling from one foot to the other and crying while Stevie held me – and it's weird, because even now when I hear that verse of that song in a bar or club, I immediately feel about four inches tall.

Eventually, the police came back over and told me that there was nothing they could do. The photograph, they said, was 'not a graphic image' because I had underwear on. They guessed that if I hadn't been wearing it, it would have been a different story. Finally, they reassured me that they'd made him delete the picture. Great, I thought.

That's one less person who has a picture of my vagina. If I'd been in less of a state I would have realised that my evidence had just been deleted. They ushered us back into the festival and Stevie asked if I wanted to leave. I didn't want to ruin the entire day, so I said no. We stayed and tried to enjoy the rest of the gig. To anyone else it would have looked like I was having a great time, but denial is a very funny thing. It was easy to pretend – because I wanted it all to be okay – but I couldn't push what had happened to the back of my mind. I felt weird, humiliated and violated, and what's worse, I knew the guys who'd done this to me were probably having a great night. When I look back now I understand how I was behaving. As women, we are so used to putting up with and brushing off harassment, intimidation, assault or worse. We feel it's our fault and we're scared of causing a fuss. And I, dancing away after this had just happened, was the embodiment of that. Of just 'getting on with it'.

Four days later I was heading to Latitude Festival for a job. It was super last minute and I threw a bunch of clothes in a bag. While getting ready, I picked up a skirt, and decided against packing it, but eventually, urged by my boyfriend, and in a mini act of defiance, I took it along and swore to wear it. On the way to the festival, I received a call from the Met Police. A tired and emotionless voice told me that my case was closed and nothing else would be done. I hung up, and I swear to god something inside of me snapped. This concoction of anger, dismay and defiance simmered in my belly. I'd put up with guys smacking my arse, shouting at me in the street and screaming disgusting stuff at me from cars for years. I'd worn headphones to avoid the comments, carried keys between my fingers at night, avoided the underpass – built to save my life from oncoming traffic. I'd made up having a boyfriend because 'no' was never enough in clubs. I'd laughed when a security guard – employed to protect me when I worked in a rowdy student bar – felt my boobs to 'see if I was wearing a stab-proof vest'. I'd told no one when a man on the tube rested his open hand firmly on my right bum cheek from Camden Town to Euston during the rush-hour crush. I'd ignored it when my boyfriend's boss showed everyone at his work a photo of my legs and then asked my boyfriend if he could help 'show Gina what a real man is'. I'd seen how men's eyes had deepened and suddenly looked at me differently when I'd turned sixteen, and I'd pushed it aside when guys in bars had moved to grind their crotches against my backside without any warning. I'd been sexualised without my consent for as long as I could remember, and I was fucking over it. I was over accepting it as 'part of life' – as part of my fee for being born a woman. So this time, I thought, I'll talk about it. Surely it didn't have to be 'part of life'. *Surely* I deserved more than this bullshit constantly? I was sick of putting on an act. I was exhausted. I was done.

12 February 2019: The Voyeurism Act

Me, my boyfriend, my lawyer Ryan and my family – including my auntie, who flew in from Spain – were cramped in the tiny gallery seats in the balcony at the House of Lords. We overlooked the full house as Baroness Chakrabarti spoke on the campaign and the bill, and there was a small silence before I heard Lord Keen of Elie speak the words 'Bill passed'. I just smiled quietly. In my head I tried to tell myself I'd 'done it', but it didn't work. We'd been here before – in the gallery watching every stage of our bills – for months. We had met with countless MPs in this building, held events that educated politicians on the bill and lobbied the government here for eighteen months. So this time, my brain still told me it was part of the process. Except it wasn't. It was the *end* of the process. We quietly shuffled out of the gallery and into the tiny wooden halls that led to the House. As I walked through the doorway my mum was standing there waiting for me. She grabbed my face with both her hands and looked directly into my eyes, her own huge green eyes full of tears, her chin wobbling as she shook her head. She just held me there for a second and I could literally see everything she wanted to say in her face. She was so unbelievably proud of me. But there was this real maternal and undeniable relief for me, relief that I'd been able to finish it. That I'd triumphed and that I'd won. I smiled and hugged her. I hugged Ryan. He said, 'I told you we'd do it.' We all exited the Houses

8

of Parliament, walking past the throngs of angry Brexit protesters, and found a little old local pub. For the rest of the evening, the eight of us sat in the corner of this dimly lit pub, drank red wine and talked and laughed. Once the wine had diluted some of the intense numbness I was feeling, I began to cry, and my boyfriend cradled me, rocking me back and forwards and smiling with pride. My cousin caught it on camera and now I still see it as the only moment I really realised what I had achieved. At 1am we drunkenly bundled ourselves into taxis and headed to my house where we tucked into pizzas, danced to records and talked until 3am. We had done it.

Let's turn the clock back to July 2017, a couple of days after I was upskirted. I met my friend Giselle Wainwright – who was then the deputy editor of the now defunct *Look* magazine – and told her what had happened. Giselle asked me to write my story for her and for that I am truly grateful – her offer gave me a voice and writing the piece felt like taking action. I was doing something proactive to challenge what had happened to me. I did some research for the piece and poured my heart into writing it, giving the assault a new name: upskirting. This was no longer a 'type of photograph' but an insidious form of violation, and the name needed to reflect that. A week later, the piece was published and I received a handful of messages from women and girls telling me that the same thing had happened to them. At that point, I had no idea these messages would become part of my everyday life for the next eighteen months.

As soon as I read those first few messages, I wanted to do more. I threw myself deeper into researching 'upskirt photos' and hundreds of thousands of porn sites glorifying non-consensual creepshots of women and children flooded my screen. When I headed to the Mail Online website, reams of pictures of female celebrities getting out of taxis popped up. It was clear paparazzi had positioned themselves in exactly the right place to capture whatever they could, non-consensually, of these women's bodies. This had been normalised since before I could remember. I found out that photographers were paid up to four times more than usual to get these types of shots. I'd seen this in every tabloid growing up – lining the shelves of the supermarkets my family shopped in, and at the newsagents I used to go to for sweets after school, but I'd never been upset or disgusted by it. This consumption of women's bodies without their consent was insidious and common, and didn't outrage me because of exactly that. It was normal. As I scrolled through pages and pages of Google I was totally struck by how many pap shots and porn sites there were, but commentary on it as a form of harassment? Nowhere to be seen. No one was talking about this. So, I wondered if there were any specific rules against it. I began researching the law in the UK and came across a few write-ups that suggested that although taking a video or photos under someone's skirt without their consent had been illegal in Scotland for almost a decade, it wasn't a sexual offence in England and Wales. I couldn't believe this. I thought I must have been wrong so I told a friend of mine, Natasha – a law student – what I thought I'd uncovered and asked her to look into the law. She came back to me days later with a one-pager that confirmed my suspicions. There was, quite obviously, a gap in the law. If you were upskirted in a private place like a bathroom or changing room, you could prosecute under the charge of voyeurism, but if it happened to you in a public place, it was far more difficult to prosecute and many instances didn't fall under any law.

Essentially, you could only prosecute with a 100-year-old public nuisance order under the charge of 'outraging public decency'. This is a common law offence that charges people for subjecting the public to seeing something lewd or crude – like urinating at a festival – but completely fails to recognise that upskirting was an offence targeting a victim, not the public. There was also a list of specifics you had to satisfy to be able to prosecute, which many instances of upskirting would not meet. One, for example, was that there had to be two or more people there to see the lewd act happen. It dawned on me that for the few women who had been brave enough to report this type of assault, prosecutors – up until now – had often had to slap a public nuisance order on the sexual offence and it just didn't fit. I immediately understood why the police hadn't prioritised my case: it wasn't that they didn't care, they were simply confused as to what they could do, or if they knew of the offence of outraging public decency, they thought it was a huge amount of work for probably no return.

At this point in my life I was working full-time in a small advertising agency as a copywriter and I knew how to use social media, so I uploaded a selfie my sister and I had taken before I had been upskirted that happened to have my two perpetrators in the background. I circled their heads and asked people to share so we could find out who these guys were and hold them accountable. I wanted to do something about this. The post went a little bit viral and then Facebook deleted it, getting in touch with me to cite 'harassment' as the reason. Me posting a photograph of these men's faces was harassment, but apparently them taking photos of my crotch, without my consent, and sending them around was not. I was incandescent with rage.

A week after this moment, while on a phone call to my boyfriend, I decided that I wanted to try and change the law. However, I had no bloody idea where to start. I limply googled 'how to change the law' and, of course, nothing useful came up. In that moment, I realised I was going to have to work this out for myself. For the next few weeks I researched other campaigns and thought hard about my approach. Then, in August 2017, I launched a national campaign to make upskirting a sexual offence in England and Wales, with no experience and no real clue what I was doing. Alongside my full-time job, I pushed news producers to book me, pitched my story to websites and even did live TV debates opposite police officers who told me the solution was to wear trousers. I emailed prosecutors, lawyers and police commissioners, set up a petition and ran sponsored Facebook ads that all asked one question: 'Why is upskirting not a sexual offence?' After months of online abuse and more media than I could handle, I realised that if I was going to fight the law and lobby the government, I needed a lawyer – but I had zero money. I found out about pro-bono law support through research and set about looking for representation. Eventually, I found Ryan Whelan. He was twenty-nine, passionate about justice, impressed by my work up until that point and knew I had a solid argument. He was also, critically, keen to help for the right reasons. We cared about the same things, and he was offering anything he could do to help me. This was not an ego trip for him or a 'project', it was a passion. We became campaign partners, and began planning our strategy and political campaign, which we ran, and worked on, every single day for eighteen months. This campaign was the single hardest, testing and most complex thing I've ever done. From ripping myself out of bed at 5am more times than I care to remember, to learning about the political system and working out how to think strategically, to pushing through serious fear and mentally switching between my job in advertising and the work with Ryan, it was 553 days of exhaustive work. And a mission that involved more passion and more purpose than I've ever experienced in my life.

The truth is, we live in a frantic political climate: a reality TV star is President of the USA, swathes of the powerful elite have been outed as exploitative and abusive by the #MeToo movement and Brexit is a mess. Sure, this may be deflating and depressing to think about, but the reality is there's never been a better time to roll up our fucking sleeves and push to make society better. Now is the moment to be passionate about making the world better for everyone. Now is the most crucial time to *be the change*. Social media has given us never-before-had access to those who run the country. We have more opportunities than ever before to engage and hold people accountable. Plus, the platforms we use to do that have become our most valuable tools in forcing change – all we need is someone to take a moment to show us how to leverage them. I'm living proof of that.

Without any political or legal experience, I have changed the law. Me! A regular, working-class person with a full-time job. I got very mediocre grades in school and I always said the only industry I'd refuse to go into was politics. I'm also so spectacularly disorganised that in the last decade I've lost twenty debit cards. If I can change the law, you can too. If you think about it, activism is pretty simple: you identify something that bothers you and you try to fix it. But you don't have to go straight to the top and try to change the law, you can make vital change on a micro-level too. Your issue can be something you've experienced, or even a small part of a big issue you care about. Are you done with seeing everyone wearing wasteful fast-fashion? Create a clothes-swap initiative. Do you want to change the conversation around representation? Organise a stunt. If you care about ecological issues, start a fundraiser. You see, changing things isn't a feat only accomplished by what we consider remarkable people, it's a goal that's doable if you have a bit of self-belief, determination and knowhow. And that's why I'm writing this book. I want you to know what campaigning is really like and how to kick ass at it. The very fact that you chose this book among all others and want to spend time here with me speaks volumes; you are already someone who wants to make the world a better place, and that's pretty remarkable. We need more people like you.

That interest in society's progression is the only thing you can't teach. Passion for change is all you need. Everything else you can learn as you go! There is no limit to what you can learn and achieve, and hopefully I can be the catalyst for that. By the time you've turned the last page of this book, you should feel ready to take on the world. I'll walk you through everything I've learned campaigning, teaching you every trick I picked up along the way. Whatever you want to fight for, this will be a supportive and helpful place to get started. Whether you need something to dip into to keep you on track, or you want to plan a campaign from start to finish but have no idea where to begin, it's all here. No jargon, no bullshit, just honest, practical advice and some of the tough (and embarrassing) lessons I've learnt the hard way. How do you get a lawyer when you don't have any money? How do you get into the right spaces with the people who have the power to help? How do you take an online campaign offline? From starting out to seeing it through to the end, this is the definitive toolkit for enforcing change. Because if I can do it, then my god so can you. Let's do this.

HOW TO USE
THIS TOOLKIT

F rom this book you will learn:

- What activism really is and why it's so important
- How to use the internet to aid your passions
- How to think more strategically
- How to figure out what you care about
- How to do the hardest thing in activism: start

I wrote this book for you. It's not about me and how I changed the law. It's your roadmap, your toolkit and your guide to getting started and pushing for what you think is right. Whether you read it from start to finish, or keep it close and dip in and out of it along the journey, it's here to make you feel ready, more confident, and to help you kick-start a campaign, initiative, movement or idea. I have never been someone who wants to keep my cards close to my chest, and with this kind of work, it's so bloody import-ant that I communicate everything I've learnt so far to you so that you can get started making the world a better place, too. I don't want you to be precious about this book. Fill out the questions. Make notes, draw diagrams, make it yours. Go back and repeat stages if you need to, skip bits you don't need right now; campaigning and activism aren't linear and so using this book doesn't have to be either. And because I want to always be honest, I want you to know I don't have all the answers here. Can I tell you a lot of stuff you can't find on Google? Sure. But my work is my work, and there'll be wisdom you'll find along the way that I just haven't hit on. Add it to this book. Make notes, add quotes. Make these pages an encouraging and useful place to be. I hope this helps. I hope you feel inspired after reading it.

Section One

ACTIVISM 101

1

WHAT MAKES
AN ACTIVIST?

*⁶ How wonderful it is that nobody need wait
a single moment before starting to improve
the world.⁹*

Anne Frank

activist
/ˈaktɪvɪst/
noun
A person who campaigns to bring about political or social change.

When something makes you feel uncomfortable,
human instinct is to hide, to shy away from confron-
tation and to get back to safe, comfortable, ordinary life.

And listen, I'm not talking about self-preservation here. If you need – for your mental health or otherwise – to lie low and look after yourself, do it. Here, I am talking about the tendency to retreat due to feeling defeated by the system: an innate sense of powerlessness. Of not rocking the boat. When every option other than ignoring it seems complicated, big and messy, or impossible. It's that automatic self-assessment of inadequacy that I want to address, because I felt it. This felt far too big for me to achieve, and questioning the status quo felt scary. I remember standing at the exit to a tube station on a cold, grey London day, speaking to my boyfriend on the phone about my upskirting experience. He said, 'Well, you could ignore it, sure. But imagine if you fought it. I know you're saying something should be done about this but what if *you* did it? What if *you* changed the law?' For a second I considered it. It felt huge, lofty, brilliant, and therefore not for me. It was far too big and way too hard for little old me to ever accomplish. I think I actually just laughed at him and shook my head, and as I exited the tube, the same old subconscious thoughts came into play: 'I wouldn't be able to do it anyway.' Well, actually buddy, you have zero basis for that response. Show me the evidence that says you can't.

WHY ANYONE CAN DO IT

Unless you are an extraordinarily privileged white male from vast, inherited wealth and a powerful family, the chances are you probably won't automatically assume that you have a stake in the decisions that shape our world, or the right to challenge those decisions when you believe they are unjust. Too much of the information fed to us throughout our lives makes us think otherwise, because it's way easier for those in power if we are apathetic and just sit back and let them run the show. You see, we learn about power and hierarchy via a million subliminal messages fed to us by the media, services and institutions we spend time with every single day, and although we may know we're part of a community, and understand on some level that our behaviour can change our immediate surroundings, we often feel more like the pieces of a puzzle rather than the one putting together those pieces. The thing is, I'm done with that way of thinking. I'm over it. It's time to realise that *normal everyday people know, truly, what matters most. Normal, everyday people hold the key to change because they understand, more than anyone, what needs to change. They see it and live it, day in, day out.*

I mean, Jesus, it's the biggest dupe ever. Somehow, the public have been convinced that they aren't the people to do the job of 'changing things'. Somehow the powerful have convinced the very people holding the evidence that they'd have no power to influence the jury. But truthfully? We do hold the power. And successful activists know it. The most decorated change-makers often go back to their roots so that they can understand and observe, with new clarity, what needs to change. Even Nobel Peace Prize winner Kailash Satyarthi said he needs to keep connected with his community to know his work is on the right track: 'Being directly connected with ordinary people gives me much more confidence in what I am trying to do.'* So when it comes down to it, being a normal person and having the ability to recognise and understand what needs to change on a fundamental level is critical. Because it's how activism starts, and, as we all know, starting is the hardest part.

So many of us are born with privilege, in myriad forms, and although the ability and belief necessary to make change is heavily (I repeat: heavily) informed by privilege, there is not one 'type' of person who can make change, and one who can't. There is no recipe for an activist. It's the one thing we all have in common: we are all capable of making our societies, and therefore our world, a better place. All of us. For too long, we've allowed that power to fall into the hands of a select few – I don't buy that as a necessarily effective or fair way to run things and neither should you.

Generally activism is about advocacy work, campaigning and social disobedience undertaken to shake up the current system with the aim of creating real, tangible and systemic social, economic or political change. It sounds like serious stuff, and it is. So, surely it's only work undertaken by serious, effective, productive people, right?

That's what I thought. Before I started my work as an

_____

* Kailash Satyarthi in interview with Mary de Sousa, 'Kailash Satyarthi: Fighting for children's rights, one step at a time', UNESCO website, https://en.unesco.org/courier/january-march-2018/kailash-satyarthi-fighting-children-s-rights-one-step-time (accessed March 2019).

activist, the word would immediately conjure up for me someone that made me feel very *very* bad about myself: a strong and remarkable character who was born to change things. Someone just born to be *someone*. When they started walking and talking it was immediately obvious that they were exceptional; an individual who knew exactly who they were. They were born with fire in their belly, a plan and an unwavering sense of purpose. As an adult, they are highly effective, charismatic, organised and get out of bed at 5am without an issue. And they don't eat hummus with their fingers. Y'know, *that* kind of person.

The truth? An activist isn't actually any one 'kind' of person. They're not a breed. They're not homogeneous. We are all activists in training. We're learning about the world all the time, and all at different levels. Sure, certain personality traits may make becoming an activist an easier mission, but the kind of people who have forced change through history have a skillset as varied as any other kind, and not every activist is a 'remarkable' person. Let's take the activist I know best as an example: good ol' me. Some personality traits that helped me start and become successful in my activism are: my empathy for others, my stubbornness (finally it was good for something), being a good communicator and my determination (see: stubbornness). But, like all of us, I am chock-full of traits that did *not* help. Traits that I had to desperately control for fear of them derailing my efforts altogether. One of these is my incredibly poor practical skills; I struggle more than most on a daily basis to organise and function as an effective adult who's 'on top of things'. I've been known to turn up to events on the wrong date (seriously), I cannot for the fucking life of me get out of bed in the morning without feeling personally attacked, and to the frustration of my partner, I am constantly forgetting to do things, booking the wrong tickets and losing everything. This annoyingly, but naturally, transfers to my work, so upkeep, administration and follow-through on projects are a constant slog for me and I have to literally force and incentivise myself, like I'm a seven-year-old, to complete tasks. With activism this is a nightmare because there's always multiple work streams that have to run parallel to one another, so when you're super disorganised it's a huge struggle to keep everything running smoothly. Another trait that hinders my work – yet fits together perfectly with my poor practical skills (joy!) – is my lack of focus. I find it so hard to focus on one thing. My attention span is abysmal, so I'll flit between projects and tasks for hours before settling unless I force myself to CONCENTRATE, GINA. This means that self-motivation and accountability with myself is very tough. Now, the reason I'm getting all 'Dear Diary' here is because it's important that you know whatever your 'weaknesses' are, they do *not* negate your ability to enact real and tangible change, the only thing that does is you thinking they do. Like anything else in life, it's all about doing your best.

Having said all that, there *is* one thing that elevates someone from being a civilian to the role of activist, one thing stands between the 'you' you are now and the 'you' that makes shit happen: the decision to take action. That's it. It's the golden bullet. No magical personality trait, no remarkable breaking point, just concluding that, this time, it's going to be you who tries to change something – whether big or small – instead of asking someone else to do it. As the famous saying goes, 'If not me, then who?' The remarkable beauty of making this decision is that anyone can make it – and there's nothing else quite like that. Most jobs we embark on in life have some sort of pre-requisite or requirement that we have to complete before we can get stuck in and claim the title. There is always a box to tick. Think about starting a new job, investing, buying something valuable, volunteering or even medical decisions about your own body; all of them require you to prove yourself before you begin. But activism? Nah. It's a free-for-all. A democratic buffet. It's yours. Whether you want to perform a simple act, launch a huge campaign or create some sort of slow-burning educational movement, it's your decision, on your time, and you run the show. You don't have to be 'someone' or 'something' before you can make a difference. No one can tell you you're not the right person to make the world a better place.

I'd like to quickly introduce you to a few of my favourite change-makers. These are bright, bold and passionate people – some you may know, and some you may not – who pushed, or are pushing, for change, so we can enjoy, or build on, the privileges and rights we have today. Some of them we stand on the shoulders of, and some of them we will watch grow and shape our society today. Remember while reading, though, that each and every one of these remarkable individuals started out just like you and me. They prove, to me, that change isn't only achieved by MPs, presidents, lords or judges, and that some of the most effective and awe-inspiring change has been achieved by normal, everyday folk, who didn't start off remarkable, but became remarkable by trying. This is, of course, only a handful of the very many incredible and inspiring people from throughout history and the present day that I could have chosen. These are the people who inspire me, and I hope they'll do the same for you.

CHANGE-MAKERS WHO GOT US HERE

Gloria Steinem, US feminist and political activist, 1934–present

> *The first problem for all of us, men and women, is not to learn, but to unlearn.*

Gloria Steinem is a name you'll hear during most discussions about women's rights. In the sixties she was one of the trailblazers of the feminist movement – heralded as the poster girl of Female Power. Today, as often happens with feminist icons, the landscape has changed and some of her comments and views have aged and become outdated. But her role in women's liberation and the trajectory of feminism is undeniable – and important – when considering how a normal person can enact change. Gloria grew up living between Michigan and Florida, unable to attend school properly until she was eleven. She finally settled in one place and spent the majority of her formative years living in a trailer and struggling to care for her mother Ruth, who suffered from mental illness in a time when it was misunderstood and heavily stigmatised. Eventually, Gloria headed to Smith College to study Politics and Government – a pretty unusual choice for a woman in the fifties, sure, but Gloria knew early on that she wanted to carve out her own life path; she wasn't content with a life that consisted of only marriage and motherhood. After finishing her degree in 1956, Gloria worked for an independent research centre before setting out on her own as a freelance writer, penning controversial and pioneering editorial pieces such as her undercover exposé on New York City's Playboy Club, where she posed as a Playboy Bunny – still, to this day, she's referred to as an 'ex Playboy Playmate', a reductive and absurd title that shows us how much work there is still left to do. After years of writing and finding her voice, Gloria became a regular contributor to *New York Magazine* and co-founded *Ms.* magazine. She also launched a pioneering women's organisation and started a political career that culminated in six bestselling books exploring the female experience and violence against women. All this from a young girl born into an ordinary environment and a low-income fractured family. Someone, in fact, who grew up like many of us.

Be more Gloria: Understand and admit to your growth. Things you thought were concrete will merge and change as your work takes shape and as time goes by, especially if you are working on something for a number of years, or plan to commit a portion of your life to a cause. As a life-long activist, in whatever form, your work is never done and your education never complete because society is always shifting and evolving. You will never know everything. Remember this above all.

Eileen Conn, Peckham activist and founder of Peckham Vision, 1942–present

> Don't give up when the formal procedures say it's the end. We have proved it over and over again: it's not the case. Just don't give up.

Eileen is a veteran in community activism and someone I only discovered recently. Though she's still a huge part of London's future, her work has truly led us to the London we know and love today. Eileen is almost solely responsible for ensuring that south-east London's diverse cultural hub Peckham avoids over-gentrification – the perfect example of how one person can defend their community. Without her steadfast determination over the last thirty years, work/ lifestyle space Peckham Levels (formerly a multi-storey car park) wouldn't exist, and neither would the borough's iconic music venue, the Bussey Building. Peckham Vision, the small and informal group of volunteers Eileen founded, has saved so many of Peckham's most-loved spaces. She may have been awarded an MBE for services to her community in 2009 but she's one of us – living in the same modest south London home since 1973, and going about her daily life as normal, while kicking ass and defending her neighbourhood against The Man.

> **Be more Eileen:** Stay close to your roots. You can still achieve monumental change if you stick close to home. Not every activist has to take on global organisations or head straight to Parliament. People need their communities to be nurtured and protected just as much as their rights.

Kailash Satyarthi, Indian children's rights activist, 1954–present

> ❝ I want to say that you should follow your heart, and the mind will follow you. Believe in yourself, and you will create miracles. ❞

To give Kailash the title of activist seems almost reductive. The seed for his life's work was planted when he was just five years old and witnessed a child in terrible poverty. 'The very first day of my schooling, I saw a boy, around the same age as me, sitting outside the school and looking at my shoes. He had a shoe-polishing box in front of him. I was very disturbed. My question to the teacher was: why was the boy outside and not inside the school?'* The father of the young boy went on to tell Kailash that 'People like you are born to go to school and people like us are born to work.' This stuck with him through his young adult life: he completed an electrical engineering degree, quit his job and became a teacher in his home district of Madhya Pradesh, India. Eventually he knew that he wanted to take an even more active role in changing kids' lives and in 1980 launched a campaign to bring the issues of child slave labour, trafficking and lack of education in India to attention. Without the ease of the internet, Kailash campaigned tirelessly. Kailash had his work cut out changing perceptions, so in 1980 he founded the BBA, India's largest movement campaigning for the rights of children, immediately realising that none of the United Nations bodies (UNICEF or the International Labour Organisation) had the legal power to stop children being forced into labour, trafficking, prostitution or other horrific circumstances. He was going to have to do this himself, so he set out his goal of creating an international law against child slavery. Today, Kailash has saved over 80,000 children from forced labour, won the Nobel Peace Prize in 2014, inspired India's biggest ever rallies and marches, and founded a pioneering human-rights convention – Convention 182 – which

---

* Kailash Satyarthi in interview with Mary de Sousa, 'Kailash Satyarthi: Fighting for children's rights, one step at a time', UNESCO website, https:// en.unesco.org/courier/january-march-2018/kailash-satyarthi-fighting-children-s-rights-one-step-time (accessed March 2019).

changes how people view, and work to put an end to, child labour. It has since been unanimously adopted by 181 countries. Kailash's efforts are a positive reminder that activism isn't a quick fix. It can take years and years of work, but the work is life-affirming, celebrated and makes a difference. Two for you Kailash – you go Kailash!

> **Be more Kailash:** Remember that activism is a long road. You might not get results right away. It took me just under two years, which is very quick, but that's not the case for everyone – especially if you're tackling something very complex. Progress is still progress, and the longer it takes, the more minds you're changing and the more awareness you're creating, which is just as valuable as tangible change.

Ella Baker, civil rights activist and behind-the-scenes organiser, 1903–1986

> 6 *Oppressed people, whatever their level of formal education, have the ability to understand and interpret the world around them, to see the world for what it is, and move to transform it.* 9

African-American civil rights and human rights activist Ella Baker was one of the most prolific behind-the-scenes organisers in the game. But before she was inspiring and guiding some of the world's greatest leaders, she was just a regular girl from Virginia. Growing up, Ella would listen to her grandmother's accounts of slaves rising up and revolting against their owners in America. Ella's grandmother had been born into slavery and had been physically abused for bravely refusing to marry the man her slave-owner had chosen for her. Her grandmother's stories were Ella's first education about the oppression of her people, something that would define her purpose, and she wanted to be on the right side of history in trying to address it. She headed to the state capital school in North Carolina, which was a historically black university, and graduated as class valedictorian in 1927. As a student, Ella had challenged school policies she thought were unfair, including 'the school's conservative dress code ... the paternalistic racism of its president ... and its methods of teaching religion and the Bible.'*

She moved to New York City after graduation, at a time when many people of colour were leaving the South to escape violent oppression, and went on to found the first Negro History Club at the Harlem Library, and she regularly attended lectures and meetings at the YMCA. Ella played a huge role in some of the most iconic and influential organisations of the time, including the National Association for the Advancement of Colored People (NAACP), Martin Luther King's Southern Christian

---

* Barbara Ransby, *Ella Baker and the Black Freedom Movement: A Radical Democratic Vision*, Chapel Hill: University of North Carolina Press, 2003, p. 59.

Leadership Conference, and the Student Nonviolent Coordinating Committee. A true example of someone who shows up for their community.

> **Be more Ella:** Start small, and invest in your community. Is there something in your school or local community you think is unfair? Could you challenge them on that if you secure backing from others? And when you're in a position to challenge bigger injustices, always keep close contact with the community you are representing. Invest your time and help by doing like Ella and tell your story, get involved in workshops and give back.

MODERN-DAY ACTIVISTS YOU SHOULD KNOW

Malala Yousafzai, activist for female education and the youngest ever Nobel Prize laureate (@malala)

> *We realise the importance of our voices only when we are silenced.*

Head up to Oxford and you'll find modern-day human rights heroine Malala Yousafzai studying to change our world as we know it. Malala's fight began when, as a regular civilian caught in a war zone at age ten, she began chronicling her experience on a blog. After the Taliban shut girls' schools in Mingora, Pakistan, and forbade them from learning, Malala spoke out online, and was asked to be part of a BBC documentary after one of the producers spotted her blog. Fast-forward months later and, while on the bus home from taking an exam, Malala was shot in the head at point blank range by a member of the Taliban in a violent attempt to silence her. Miraculously and fortuitously, Malala survived. The world needed her. At twenty-one years old, she has achieved incredible things: founding The Malala Fund of education for girls, speaking at the United Nations, confronting President Barack Obama on his use of drone strikes, becoming a co-recipient of the Nobel Peace Prize, the youngest ever, and publicly holding the UN accountable for needing to increase their efforts in the fight for access to education for girls. Malala is a shining example of how to turn an oppressive and dangerous situation into a positive one, and how speaking out as a civilian can bring awareness on a huge scale. The change Malala instigated was born from a simple yet terrifying decision to stand up to injustice, to refuse to accept the unfair hand she was dealt. A regular girl who decided enough was enough.

Be more Malala: Use your voice, and refuse to quit. If you believe in something and know, fundamentally, that you are right, do not sway your opinion for anyone. Activism that succeeds is bold and brave, it doesn't listen to the doubters if it knows it's right, and above all, it won't be silenced.

Richie Brave, social critic, presenter, writer and speaker (@richiebrave)

> ❦ We'll sign up to the gym and get protein
> shakes, we'll spend all this money on keeping
> our bodies okay. Why are we not looking
> after our minds? ❧

Richie Brave is an activist and ally to women who inspires me continually. As a social critic, speaker and presenter, Richie focuses on the damage toxic masculinity and the lack of awareness around mental health inflict on all genders. For Richie, his activism started in childhood. He proudly describes himself as being an emotional child, something he says is not considered a positive when it comes to men: 'With boys and men we attribute emotion to negativity and vulnerability – something we say men shouldn't be.' For him, though, his emotional availability as a child gave way to something incredibly valuable: compassion. Even though Richie grew up in what he considered a 'harsh environment', he came from a nurturing family and remembered always being a compassionate kid compared to his male peers. His need to help and protect people began when he was only six years old. Richie was physically beaten by adults who were meant to be caring for him, and he realised, in that moment, that he never wanted anyone else to feel the way he had during that situation again. At that young age, he realised he could be part of making sure that no one did, and although he was yet to know what activism even was, he was on a journey that would see him grow into a campaigner and activist whose work is rooted in compassion. As a young man Richie kicked off a decade of dedicating his work and life to his community when he volunteered in the criminal justice system helping rehabilitate domestic abusers, as well as volunteering to help children, including those with behavioural difficulties, express themselves through performing arts. The work he does is critical in pushing for a society where we view everyone as equals. I have personally had the pleasure of watching Richie talk at a 100 Women I Know event in London – one of my favourite initiatives – and his words are always eye-opening. I learnt from Richie that men aren't thriving under inequality either, and that toxic masculinity – as well as being the catalyst in the oppression of women – is a gendered curse that's raising men who become subconsciously trapped in a self-perpetuating cycle of prioritising macho strength, a lack of emotional availability and dominance over healthy communication, emotional availability and self-awareness. This leads to men dominating, and women being dominated, as well as male suicide and violence and abuse against others. Richie is a tenacious force in the unpicking of toxic masculinity, and an incredible example of how simply talking, communicating and critically examining society can inspire awareness, understanding and, ultimately, action.

Be more Richie: Remember that using anger, hurt or a harsh lesson as a motivator is fine, but try and root your work in compassion. There's very little space for change if redemption isn't an option. So when you're trying to educate people and move society forwards remember to keep empathy at the forefront. Stay connected to people.

Alexandria Ocasio-Cortez, American Democratic politician and activist (@ocasio2018 / @AOC)

> ❦ I understand the pain of working-class Americans because I have experienced the pain. ❧

Alexandria is a political force to be reckoned with. Born in New York to working-class Puerto Rican parents, she grew up in the Bronx and excelled at school, winning science and engineering awards before going on to complete a bachelor's degree in International Relations, with a minor in Economics. After a stint working as an organiser on the 2011 Bernie Sanders presidential campaign, Alexandria visited Flint, Michigan during the humanitarian clean water crisis, and North Dakota, where the controversial Dakota Access Pipeline threatened the livelihood of its residents. Seeing the kind of disasters working-class Americans were facing at the hands of major corporations, she decided to run for Congress with absolutely no corporate donations or commercial backing, canvassing locally with only a bag of flyers and an online awareness campaign. After being elected in 2018, and sworn in in early 2019, she became the youngest woman to serve in Congress in the history of the United States. Alexandria has attracted controversy due to her single-minded approach and for refusing money from all corporate donors or lobbyists. It hasn't fazed her though, and she stated that 'It's disingenuous to … pretend the sources of our money don't impact the policy we write – you just can't serve two masters.'* Alexandria supports, and is vocal about, LGBTQIA+ rights and the working class, and she draws a hard line when it comes to the need for revolutionary action in the face of devastating climate change. She is totally unafraid to push bold suggestions – exactly what we need in modern-day politics. In the UK, since women were allowed to stand for Parliament in 1918, only 489 women have been elected. Bearing in mind we have 650 MPs in the house now,† 1918 was ONE HUNDRED YEARS AGO and anyone can choose to stand at any point, that is a serious issue. Alexandria is helping to change that by inspiring a new generation of working class people, and young women of colour, demonstrating that politics is for them, that they don't need to take commercial backing and that age is no barrier to making change at the highest level.

---

* Sarah Ruiz-Grossman, 'How This Young Latina Candidate is Shaking Up A New York Congressional Race', *Huffington Post*, 4 June 2018, www. huffingtonpost.com/entry/ocasio-congress-candidate-new-york-crowley_us_5b11c598e4b0d5e89e1fbf2b.
† For more information, see https://hansard.parliament.uk/lords/2018-02-05/debates/A07542E2-3B2C-4DC3-B727-B9A9FA786717/RoleOfWomenInPublicLife (accessed March 2019).

Be more Alexandria: Do things your way and stick to your convictions. Get creative if you don't have any money for your campaign: why not ask to be featured on larger platforms? Take a course on YouTube and learn to design your own branding for flyers, social media content and posters. Just like Alexandria, dress and act how you would anyway, don't compromise your personal style, identity and your roots just because you're serious about your work. We do not have to fit into boxes anymore.

Munroe Bergdorf, British model, writer and activist (@munroebergdorf)

> ❛ *If people rallied around issues that don't affect them as well as ones that do, we'd be getting shit done.* ❜

Munroe Bergdorf is a name you probably already know if you follow me on Instagram (my stories are pretty much a fan account for her), or if you are on Instagram at all. The model and trans activist has been a leading voice in the LGBTQIA+ community since L'Oréal decided to hire her, use her name to sell make-up, and then promptly fire her for expressing the stone-cold fact that racism and white supremacy are rampant today – a bad business decision if ever I saw one, but a stark reminder to marginalised communities and their allies that not all support is authentic, especially when it comes from a corporation. Since the start of her activism in 2016, Munroe has been a strong and much-needed critical voice, speaking on the topics that so many with a platform her size avoid, and flooding every musty, ugly corner of transphobia, homophobia and damaging heteronormative narratives with light, forcing straight and cis people to show up – and stand up – for the trans community. Munroe grew up just outside of Essex and Hertfordshire, her father Jamaican and her mother white British. She struggled at school: being educated at an all-boys school and being, as she refers to it, gender-queer, was a tough experience, and she would routinely deal with physical bullying. After heading to university to study fashion and working in the industry for a couple of years, Munroe began her transition and worked as a DJ internationally, becoming known for her talent and her political views. Since coming to the public's attention in 2017 during the L'Oréal controversy, Munroe's platform has grown greatly and she has harnessed its power to educate the masses. She's the perfect example of a social activist who uses social media as a critical part of her work – not an afterthought. Munroe marks a new kind of social-media personality, a purpose-led influencer who is creating social change with her content, not just pretty ads for brands.

Be more Munroe: Use the internet to lift up, and stand up for, your community and your cause. Show up for those who need you online. If you're a privileged white man or woman, show up for marginalised communities; do the work online, learn from others, then use your platform to showcase their work and what you've learnt. If there's an issue you care about, use social media to build awareness around it (more on that later), and use your voice to educate people. Awareness is half the fight and the internet can be your biggest asset, as it has been for Munroe.

Greta Thunberg, climate activist and speaker (@GretaThunberg)

> ❝ For way too long, the politicians and the people in power have gotten away with not doing anything to fight the climate crisis, but we will make sure that they will not get away with it any longer. We are striking because we have done our homework and they have not. ❞

After wildfires ravaged Sweden in the summer of 2018, fifteen-year-old Greta Thunberg – who had been convincing her family of the dangers of climate change since watching a documentary at eight years old that deeply affected her – decided to bunk off school until the 2018 Swedish general elections. Holding a sign that read 'Skolstrejk för klimatet' ('School Strike For The Climate'), and sitting outside Parliament for hours on end every Friday, she demanded, solo, that the Swedish government reduce carbon emissions in accordance with the Paris Agreement.

Locals started to notice the bundled-up young girl sitting on the pavement in the same area every Friday, and after the general elections her determination began to receive nationwide and then worldwide attention. After her profile was raised, Greta – who struggled with public speaking – decided to push through her fear and speak at TEDxStockholm on the danger of apathy when it comes to climate change, before addressing the UN and telling them, 'You have to speak clearly, no matter how difficult that may be', and that 'You say you love your children above all else, and yet you are stealing their future in front of their very eyes.' Her candid and harsh speeches addressing those in power have become infamous, and her lone strikes have now sparked a worldwide climate strike across 100 countries, with millions of children and people dedicating their time and voices to demanding more from their governments. Greta is a tiny powerhouse, and she is my hero.

Be more Greta: Pay no attention to what others are doing or whether they will join you on your journey. If you are passionate and you care, go ahead and do it anyway. Stay consistent and lead by example. The power of one is, indeed, very powerful, and you will find that starting is the most important thing. Try to push through your fears because your voice is needed.

Xiuhtezcatl Roske-Martinez, indigenous environmental activist, hip-hop artist and youth director of Earth Guardians (@xiuhtezcatl)

> ❝ *Real change must come from people, rather than the government.* ❞

Xiuhtezcatl (pronounced shoo-TEZ-caht) may be young, but he has a lifetime's worth of work behind him. The indigenous environmental activist from Colorado is the youth director of Earth Guardians and the lead plaintiff in the youth-led lawsuit against the US government for failing to protect the environment for future generations (the most badass thing I've ever heard). This guy has been on a mission to save the world since he was only six years old. After watching a nature documentary as a kid, Xiuhtezcatl was alerted to the effect of climate change and started working out how he could help. He started to write and produce his own music, calling for immediate action on climate change, campaigned to get pesticides out of his local parks, to contain the use of coal ash, and to place moratoriums on fracking in Colorado. At only thirteen, Xiuhtezcatl received the United States Community Service Award and served on President Obama's Youth Council after he was noticed for his work. In 2015, when he was fifteen, he confronted the world's apathy towards its own extinction in his speech at the United Nations when he said: 'What's at stake right now is the existence of my generation.' Xiuhtezcatl is the definition of a grassroots activist: starting locally and then pushing his way into spaces most of us wouldn't dare to enter; taking small projects and using momentum to build on each until he got into rooms with those who can help to change the world – that's how powerful people in grassroots communities can be. He shows that gaining access and gaining influence is easier than we think. In addition, Xiuhtezcatl is now a fully fledged (and painfully cool) nineteen-year-old hip-hop artist with a difference, using his music to communicate environmental and societal issues to the world. He even submitted self-produced music to the United Nations Framework Convention on Climate Change in the hope that it would 'inspire the negotiations'. His song 'Speak For The Trees' was chosen as the Jury Award Winner at the convention, and his album *Break Free* was released in March 2017.

Be more Xiuhtezcatl: Build your activism muscle instead of going in over your head and feeling out of your depth. Is there a cause in your local vicinity you could help with? Maybe your building doesn't recycle, maybe your local park isn't doing enough to protect its wildlife or maybe you've noticed discrimination in your workplace. Look at your community and see if you can better it. Starting local like Xiuhtezcatl did is a sure-fire way to change things and get your foot in the door for bigger projects. And using your talent is a great way to communicate your message.

Aja Barber, writer, author (@ajabarber)

> 66 *My message won't always make you comfortable, but it will make you think.* 99

Aja Barber is a writer, author, sustainable fashion expert and stylist, micro-blogger on Patreon and Instagram. Her work focuses on sustainability, ethics, intersectional feminism, racism and all the ways systems of power effect our buying habits. Aja is one of my favourite 'activists', although she may be hesitant to call herself that. From where I stand, everything she does is *active* and is actively pushing for justice for marginalised people; garment working, Black women, plus-sized women and more. She truly leads from love and brings a no-bullshit approach to her work that breaks things down in such a way that you don't feel overwhelmed, but feel like you get it. Aja always had an eye for, and a love of, fashion, but realised the problem with over-consumption quickly after noticing her own consumption habits. The fashion industry wasn't one that uplifted, supported or even really welcomed women who sit at the intersections she did. It's the sort of industry that won't let marginalised people walk through the front door, and as she describes "without privilege you pretty much have to crawl in through a window to get in ... ". But that's what she did; as a stylist with a focus on sustainability and a writer discussing topics and issues surrounding sustainable fashion. She would work with her clients to find second-hand luxury clothing and items that fit their brief, but didn't pump money into an unregulated industry that was hurting the world not to mention those that make the clothes. Later down the line she started microblogging and that's where I discovered her. I remember following Aja back in 2018 and learning bucket loads within months. Her Patreon is a brilliant community built around her wealth of knowledge, musings, discourse and critical thinking around colonialism, fashion, race, and the fashion industry as a whole and I've become a way more conscious consumer and a better person since I started listening to her and reading her work.

Be more Aja: Only ever punch up. Your job as someone with privilege is to collect **your community.** You could be going around collecting white people and educating them on their problematic views/behaviours and complicity in racism and other structural inequalities for the rest of your life and you'd **never** run out of people to educate. It is not your place to tell someone more marginalised than you what they could be doing better or differently. They live at intersections you can never fully understand and therefore your opinion on them isn't helpful or, oftentimes, even correct, as it lacks context. Punching down is shitty. Punching up is the only way to do the work. If you stick to this rule, you'll often be directing your energy in the right place.

WHY IT'S THE BEST THING YOU'LL EVER DO

So, we've established that some of the most important changes in history have been driven and fought for by average people like you and me; human beings who mess up and make mistakes, but who also push boundaries and refuse to sit and ignore what they know to be wrong.

However, if you were reading these bios thinking, *Jesus H Christ, Gina, this sounds like gruelling work. What's in it for me?*, then I hear you. You'd imagine that committing a good chunk of your time to making the world better for everyone else would leave you an emotionally bankrupt shell of a human, but it's quite the opposite. In my case, there are only a few feelings I can articulate about campaigning because it was such an overwhelming rollercoaster ride of an experience, but one thing I can say with complete and utter certainty is that deciding to try and change something I thought was wrong was the best decision I ever made. I have never, in my life, felt prouder of myself for the effort I put in. I've never had more purpose, something real and tangible to aim for, and I've never felt more confident in my professional ability. It's incredible how changing other people's experiences can completely transform your own, too.

Finding a cause that speaks to you and helps others is one of the most rewarding feelings in the world and a sure-fire way to develop your confidence and identity, because pushing society forward – whether in a small or big way – is the ultimate crash course. Activism teaches you life's most valuable lessons at the kind of speed, and in the kind of unexpected combinations, that will have you looking back on the previous six months, mind blown at how much you have developed. I may have pretended I was confident, bold and ready to take on the world for the first three months of my campaign – all right, fine, the first *six*. But after that? I started to actually believe in myself and my ability, because I had learnt so, so much. Although it can be a daunting task, this kind of work is illuminating at the very least and life affirming at its best. You'll see your community and society in a whole new light, develop your identity and build your self-esteem and resilience all at once. There's even an official term for the emotional benefits of forcing change: the 'activism cure'. Activism triggers the brain to release dopamine – the chemical responsible for feelings of pleasure and reward. Research from the National Institute of Mental Health (NIMH) has even found that the high from seeing your work develop can give you a hit of adrenaline, which in some cases can even alleviate physical pain. The science is there, guys. Showing up for others is good for you, and nothing will get you out of bed like the feeling that comes from activism.

2

YOUR MOMENT IS NOW

I f you're looking for a time to get into activism, *now is that time*. Research shows we're becoming more and more politically engaged: according to an Opinion study, a huge 64 per cent of young voters headed to the polls in the 2016 EU Referendum compared to the 43 per cent who voted in the general election the previous year (despite the ramifications of the former being far more complex).* The last twelve years have seen three changes of prime ministers, two of which outside the electoral process, and in the US and UK a political shift from more centralised politics to more right-leaning tendencies has led to the marked rise of identity politics – the tendency for those who belong

---

* John Burn-Murdoch, 'Youth Turnout at General Election Highest in 25 Years, Data Show', *Financial Times*, 20 June 2017, www.ft.com/content/6734cdde-550b-11e7-9fed-c19e2700005f.

to a specific religion, race or social background to start to prioritise their own movement over traditional broad-based party politics. The power of unprecedented access to information and social media as a tool for discussion, news and community has carved out alternative avenues for us to make social and political change happen, and we'd be silly not to use it. You can tell that we are starting to recognise these digital tools as a huge opportunity for change, so if you've felt more inspired and interested in social issues than ever these past couple of years you're not alone. There's a sea change happening, and we're the ones who can ride the wave.

POLITICS AND THE PEOPLE

Let's not beat around the bush here, the relationship between people and politics – namely politicians – has always been a fragile one. The imbalance of power often results in people feeling disenfranchised and disempowered, and politicians have done little to change that. According to UK market research specialists Ipsos Mori, a tiny 17 per cent of people surveyed said they trusted politicians, and the problem doesn't seem to be going away.* But should we, as citizens, expect to vote, and then sit back and implicitly trust those who run our country to solve all of society's

---

* See the table of figures at www.ipsos.com/ipsos-mori/en-uk/trust-professions-long-term-trends (accessed March 2019).

wrongs? When we vote, do we expect that crossing that one box will cause exactly what we want to happen without any extra involvement on our part, and if so, is that fair to ask? In a political utopia, maybe. But in a representative democracy, where we have the opportunity to tell those serving our country how we believe it should be run, when we're facing the reality of Brexit, catastrophic climate change and social injustices, hell no. The common person has a role to play in the complex progression of our insanely complex society. And the truth is, politics has never just been about the people working in Westminster's beautiful buildings. It's always been the process of making decisions, and the organising and managing of situations that affect a group of people or a community. It's the way we live. It's in how your workplace runs, it's in the fabric of our communities and in our friendship circles, and as soon as you realise it's about far more than just the Houses of Parliament, it becomes a lot less daunting. Politics is something the people have a role in because it is simply the way in which our society is run, and becoming part of changing that is what pushes politicians to listen and to realise what matters to the people.

The British government is now more and more an accessible part of everyday life, too, because of our good old friend the internet. Before the birth of social media, Parliament was a secretive and exclusive space that didn't feel like something we could be a part of; it felt like there was a great, gaping valley between 'the people' and the politicians, but now that gap is closing – no longer is it untouchable. Social media has democratised politics. It's levelled the playing field and the distance between politics and 'The People' is decreasing: we can find and reach those who represent us and, critically, they can see us discussing what we care about as it happens. We were once denied access to the Houses of Parliament and local council meetings, but now we can break down those walls and engage online with the very people who are running this country, our communities and our industries. But all activism doesn't have to involve engagement with the political process: it can be used to encourage social change on a local level, in a certain community or in certain power structures such as universities, offices or unions. Areas that activism can really bring value to are now way less siloed than before. Social change can happen faster, more effectively and, critically, without having to rely solely on those in power, because they can't control independent access. Previously, you would have had to rely far more on certain people for access to resources, those that could help you find information, but now you can sidestep them and build your own contacts, find resources and get information almost instantly. You control much more of the process than before. You'll notice throughout the book that I discuss 'your Gatekeeper' a lot. These people are the individuals who can help you further your cause in a big way – those who you can't get to the next stage without – and depending on what you're fighting for and how, they could be *anyone*.

As I said, politics doesn't just mean the people in the big old building in Westminster. It's how we interact as a society, which is why activism is inherently political, whether or not you're even targeting or dealing with MPs. For example, maybe you're trying to save your local library from closure – that's political. Austerity measures and decisions by the government have probably had a role to play. Maybe you're trying to ensure there are more gender options on the forms you fill in at school. Again, that's inherently political as it's about people's rights and the way our society has been informed from the top. The point is, whatever level you are fighting on, at whatever arena, and on whatever scale, activism is inherently political, and your work has the power to change the political landscape even if you're doing nothing even vaguely similar to what I did.

HOW THE INTERNET HAS CHANGED THE GAME

The very platforms that are changing the game of politics are changing themselves, too. Social justice is coming to social media. Its users are becoming far more engaged in content that has a social undercurrent, and if those platforms engage in less than helpful activity, we're calling them out. Where so many of us used to look to perfection, we're now turning to the authentic. We're seeking inspiration not just aspiration, we're using our voices more online, and we believe in the power of social media just as much as we do in marches and rallies. Youth insights consultancy Voxburner carried out a study which found that 74 per cent of millennials believe that online activism is as important as traditional activism – that spells a *huge* opportunity, and sense of urgency.* All you need to do is take a look at the #MeToo movement founded by Tarana Burke to see a hunger for change and a collective lack of patience shifting how we use modern online culture. The viral sensation calling out sexual assault took over the internet in October 2017 and became one of the largest global campaigns ever seen; to date there have been over nineteen million #MeToo tweets. A tidal wave of online conversation led to a change in attitudes offline, and incredible initiatives like Time's Up and the UK Justice and Equality Fund – who have raised millions of pounds to end the culture of harassment, abuse and impunity. Add the 'March For Our Lives' campaign against gun violence in the US and the global civil rights movement #BlackLivesMatter, and it's clear to see that we now have the tools and are ready to roll up our sleeves, use our voices and push for a more just society in our own way. Plus, our desire to do some good isn't just a hobby: Research undertaken by the Creative Artists Agency and Intern Sushi reports that 60 per cent of Gen Z 'want their jobs to impact the world for good'† showing a real and tangible commitment to change.

The truth is activism has become cool. *It's cool to do good.* My campaign may not have done half as well had it started

---

* Lea Legraien, 'Generation Quiet: Why Millennials are Rejecting the Outdoor Protest', the *Independent*, 2 February 2017, www.independent. co.uk/student/student-life/millennials-generation-y-quie-polite-activism-protest-streets-activism-twitter-facebook-ice-bucket-a7559801.html.
† Rick Wartzman, 'Coming Soon to Your Office: Gen Z', *TIME*, 12 February 2014, http://time.com/6693/coming-soon-to-your-office-gen-z/.

in 2006. People are open to change because there is so much political and social unrest, and creative communities online are making the language, look, feel and purpose of activism sound more commercial and inclusive than it ever has. Forget fist-in-the-air cold hard revolution vibes, new age activism is all about being yourself, doing what you believe in and not taking any shit. Take me, for instance. I chose specifically not to change the way I dressed when I began attending the Houses of Parliament regularly. I didn't want to have to reduce my colourful, playful femininity because I was in a black-and-white, suited-and-booted male-dominated environment, and the empowering youth-led landscape I'm part of made me feel like I didn't have to. Modern-day activism has no 'look', it's about individuals. It's about people. However you look, however you dress and whoever you are, activism is for you.

THE HUMAN STORY

There is one thing that has galvanised the public like nothing else in every campaign, every movement and every effort since activism began: the human story. But now, the human story has even more power. There will never be anything more effective than putting yourself in someone else's shoes to get you motivated, and in an era of identity politics and segregation, more than ever, we are looking for the human behind the stories we read, the businesses we buy from and the TV we watch. We view our commercial sector very differently from how our parents did. For example, there has been a sea change in attitudes towards the commercial sector since the 1990s. We're no longer happy to give money to huge, faceless corporations, and the pejorative connotations of capitalism persist in online discussions of consumerism. With the birth of social media, the outrage and action is immediate and more damaging for a brand than ever. We've begun to ask more of our advertisers, of our stores and of our industries, because we now know about the ecological issues we're facing, the horrific reality of slave labour in fast-fashion and the greed and short-sightedness that led to the economic collapse. There has always been a low grumble of disdain for the big banks, the fashion houses and the supermarkets, but now that grumble has turned into everyday consumer action and many of us are increasingly looking for the human touch when parting with our hard-earned cash – a fact mirrored by the news that UK small businesses increased by 197,000 during 2017.* With this in mind, it's clear to see why big brand activism is still a contentious endeavour. We want to see a human – and a fallible one at that – fighting for causes, not multi-million-pound businesses which have spent hundreds of thousands producing marketing that uses social justice as a way to get us to buy their products. And that change doesn't stop at the high street – look at TV entertainment. The popularity of reality TV shows

---

* https://assets.publishing.service.gov.uk/government/uploads/system/uploads/attachment_data/file/663235/bpe_2017_statistical_release.pdf

and vlogging demonstrates our interest in regular people. According to Dr Jana Scrivani, a licensed clinical psychologist, reality TV, and the regular people whose stories we watch, can be addictive because 'over time, we come to see the folks portrayed on the screen as friends. We identify with their struggles and triumphs'.* We're less and less interested in seeing infallible characters and feel far better seeing our own lives and situations reflected in the media. There's a general shift towards the real and the human, and activism is no different. We want to see people like us fight for the issues that people like us have to deal with, and we want to back people we can trust.

In the last decade, the ability to share our stories with vast swathes of people (who would otherwise never have known we exist) has changed the way we metabolise information. We now want a detailed story if we're going to give our support – we're so used to receiving information about others that we want to know what we're giving to and why it matters; the world is crying out for more average Joes and Joannes and doesn't really care for the likes of Philip Green selling 'We Should All Be Feminists' tees whilst simultaneously destroying a feminist charity pop-up. We've been burnt too many times by the Big Dogs and instead want to hear from the 'normals', people who have been through something. When all's said and done, we just want to see the little guy give it a go.

---

* For more information, see https://hellogiggles.com/reviews-coverage/tv-shows/science-behind-watching-reality-shows/ (accessed March 2019).

I believe there were two reasons why my campaign in particular was successful. Firstly, it was the classic David and Goliath story – the little one (me) taking on the big one (politicians). People didn't care if I succeeded and changed the law, they didn't put pressure on me to do that, they just wanted to see me try because seeing a regular person give it a go made them feel good. Secondly, it was my story. The story belonged to me, had happened to me, and no one else could really explain how it felt better than me. If I had been fighting for something I had no experience of, you can bet people would have disengaged (and been rightly annoyed) very quickly. We respond to people who are passionate, and nothing creates passion like personal experience. The human story was the heart of my campaign – it kept people interested long after they learned what the issue was and what I was fighting for. So whatever you want to fight for, remember people want to see it. If you want to change something in your school or university, the chances are your peers will be supportive because they want to see someone like them standing up for their rights. If you want to stop something happening in your apartment block, the residents living there with you will most likely be happy to see someone like them trying to change things for the better. Nowadays, using your experience and your story is a bigger weapon than ever before, because in the age of social media, with the decline in capitalism and, well, the rise of men like Trump, we are crying out for 'people power', and the human story has the opportunity to thrive, galvanise and engage us in a big way.

3

PEOPLE POWER: WAYS TO MAKE CHANGE HAPPEN

❛ Do it! What are you waiting on? Do it! Stand up for what you believe in. The world needs your voice. Whoever you are, you have something to say. Say it. ❜

Kerry Washington

If you're reading this right now and thinking the only way you can make an impact is by throwing yourself in head-first and launching a full-blown large-scale campaign, then stop right there. You're dead wrong. Activism isn't measured by the size of the act, but the act itself. It's about *taking* positive action that makes a difference, regardless of how big. Any act that means you're putting your time, energy, effort or money into a cause is incredibly valuable, and the sooner you realise you have far more to effect change in your arsenal than you thought, you can get out there and start effecting change. So, with that in mind, and to save you googling your arse off, here are a few easy yet powerful ways to push society forward!

THE POWER OF MONEY

When it comes to change, money is often considered king. It rules the world, much as we might sometimes wish it didn't. But cold hard cash has the ability to create opportunity, provide services and transform people's lives for the better.

Getting creative with how you use your money is the key though, and it's not *only* about donating to charity.

Every pound is a vote

The simplest and easiest way to change the world that little bit every day is by using your consumer power wisely. If you don't have the mental capacity or time to do anything else in this book right now, then do this. I know I've already gone on about faceless corporations but THEY ARE A PROBLEM, GUYS. The more money you can put into companies that have ethical, ecological or good moral missions, the better. Many independent or smaller businesses' products are more expensive than corporate convenience ones and it's a privilege to be able to choose more ethical or sustainable products over value and convenience, but if you can manage it financially, then you should be doing it. As with so many things, those who can, should. To start you off on the right path, here's a bunch of companies that make products you can swap your regular ones for and be safe in the knowledge that you're putting money into a great cause, and in doing so, asking for it to continue. It's going to be hard for you to research every single brand you give your money to – that would be a full-time job – but a great place to start is looking at a handful of the main things you buy weekly or monthly. The essentials that you know you need. Look into a handful of those companies using websites such as ethicalconsumer.org and ethicalbranddirectory. com or the Good On You app, which tells you how ethical the production of your clothes is.

Most importantly, I want you to remember one thing: being more ethical in all your purchases is overwhelming and you're going to want to give up because you're not doing it perfectly (none of us do). The most critical thing to keep in your head when trying to use your consumer power more wisely is this: we don't need a handful of people being perfect ethical consumers, we need millions doing it imperfectly.

Bulb Energy: *greener electric and gas supplier*
@bulbstagram
If you're not on green energy yet, come the hell on. There really is no excuse when it's this easy to switch. Bulb offer

100 per cent renewable electricity and 10 per cent green gas; they're pretty much the same price as any of the major energy outlets, their prices fluctuate less and they are way easier to use.

Who Gives A Crap: *sustainable toilet paper*
@whogivesacrap_tp
Bulk toilet paper delivered to your home made from 100 per cent recycled material and zero trees. Fifty per cent of their profits also go towards building toilets in disadvantaged communities.

OHNE: *organic, biodegradable tax-free tampons*
@im_OHNE
Customisable boxes of biodegradable and tax-free tampons delivered, for free, to your home each month before your period. Five per cent of revenue goes to the girls' programme run by the School Club Zambia, which organises a Menstrual Health Management programme to make sure marginalised girls and young women can better command their own potential and their bodies.

Tony's Chocolonely: *slave-free, palm-oil-free, plastic-free chocolate*
@tonyschocolonely_uk
Willy Wonka style delicious chocolate committed to social justice by paying its cocoa farmers guaranteed higher prices directly for a number of years. Plastic-free packaging, no use of palm oil and their mission is to abolish modern slavery and child labour in the chocolate industry.

LucyBee: *ethical beauty and skincare*
@lucybeecoconut
Fairtrade and palm-oil-free vegan and handmade ethical beauty and skin essentials delivered to your door. Voted most ethical skincare/beauty brand by the Ethical Consumer Survey.

plasticfreedom.co.uk: *plastic-free alternatives for cleaning, home and beauty*
*@plasticfreedom_*
Eco-friendly and plastic-free alternatives to everyday items such as fashion, food, cosmetics and cleaners that do as little harm to the environment as possible, all delivered to your door.

oddbox.co.uk: *food waste start-up*
@oddboxldn
Over 30 per cent of food produced (worth 1.3 billion tonnes) is wasted globally every year.*

Oddbox deliver wonky and rejected plastic-free fruit and veg to your home or office in cardboard boxes. Then, they donate 10 per cent of their profits to local food charities in London.

---

* Find more information here: www.fao.org/news/story/en/item/262504/icode/%20 (accessed March 2019).

Donating, fundraising and crowdfunding

This is one of the UK's favourite good acts. Donating or fundraising really is the best way to get those sweet, sugary Benjamins directly to the heart of a cause you care about. In the UK we're big givers, too: 2017 saw donations to charity rise by 600 million pounds from 2016, to make the overall sum a staggering £10.3 billion*. But again, there is a whole bunch of different ways to do this, and it's not only about the big charities.

Donating your hard-earned cash
Not sure what cause to support? Have a think about your experiences. Do you have a history of health issues in your family, and if so, could you donate monthly to research? Is one of your friends going through a tough time? Is there something you have struggled with personally that you'd like to help solve? If not, look a little outside your immediate sphere: is your community struggling with something? Why not support marginalised communities that you know are in need of the money? Could you repay women of colour for the resources and education they share online? Do any local initiatives do good work and need funding? And what about your village, town or city? Is there a problem with poverty

---

* See the Charities UK Giving March 2018 report here: www.cafonline. org/docs/default-source/about-us-publications/caf-uk-giving-2018-report. pdf (accessed March 2019).

and could you donate to local food banks? What about the elderly? Are there care homes and age initiatives you could help with? Could I ask any more questions at this point?

The point is that it's all about taking inspiration from your experience. A good tip is to do some research into which problems aren't getting as much attention as others, too. Of course, donating to big charities like Cancer Research UK or the Dogs Trust is fantastic, and important, but there are also hundreds of thousands of people donating to them each month. Maybe you could put a small percentage of your disposable income into charities or movements that have less marketing and are therefore getting less funding. Sure, it'll mean a little more hunting around, but in the end it's worth it. Witnessing the effect of your money is far more common with local, smaller charities too, and that's super rewarding. You'll actually see the change your money is making. Also, did you know that you can check how much a charity makes, where it comes from and other info by using the government's online charity register? Head to gov.uk/find-charity-information. Any charity worth its salt will appear on this list, but charities that take less than £5,000 in givings don't have to register, so remember that they might not show up, but it doesn't make them need your moolah any less!

Remember to donate directly, and without a third party so that:

- 100% of your donation goes to your chosen charity
- Your donation will be unrestricted funds, which basically means your money won't be limited to a certain project and the charity will be able to spend it on whatever needs it the most at the time
- The charity won't have had to employ someone to put together a funding bid, which is a full-time job in itself for most independent charities

Remember: If you're a UK taxpayer, always say yes to Gift Aid! It basically means that the charity can reclaim some of the tax on your donation so they'll get more than you personally donated. Think of it as the taxman adding to your donation. Win!

To get you inspired, here are some EXCELLENT independent companies to support, who are doing great work that you may not have heard of:

mermaidsuk.org.uk
@mermaidsgender
A not-for-profit charity dedicated to supporting non-binary identities outside the gender binary and cis-normativity (the assumption that all, or almost all, individuals are cisgender). They have campaigned for the recognition of gender dysphoria in young people and continually lobby for improvements in professional services. They do God's work.

fixtheglitch.org
*@glitchuk_*

A not-for-profit organisation that exists to end online abuse and #fixtheglitch, headed up and founded up by the brilliant Seyi Akiwowo (who I'm obsessed with). They offer interactive workshops that instil young people with a sense of awareness and agency when navigating the online world, as well as Digital Resilience workshop training for women either in, or thinking about stepping into, leadership roles and public appointments. This is especially important considering women are abused on Twitter every thirty seconds. I, personally, am so happy they exist.

rightsinfo.org
@rightsinfo

An independent editorial platform that fights to educate people on importance of human rights. The truth is, human rights protect us against injustice, and they make our society fairer and more equal. But the human rights system remains really fragile. Understanding of and support for human rights in the UK is low, and Rights Info's mission is to change that. These are the first guys I went to when I thought that the law was lacking, and they sent me all the information they could and supported me.

ellabakercenter.org
@ellabakercentre

Named after iconic, brilliant black hero of the civil rights movement, Ella Baker (see page 33), this independent organisation works with black, brown and low-income people to shift resources away from prisons and punishment and towards opportunities that make our communities safe, healthy and strong. They offer resources and organise people-powered campaigns to reinvest resources into communities most harmed by policing and prisons. They are completely fantastic.

lookgoodfeelbetter.com
@lgfbuk
An independent hands-on approach to tackling the physical effects of cancer, building women's confidence and providing a community for those undergoing cancer treatment. They hold free, confidence-boosting skincare and make-up workshops and masterclasses across the UK, with free make-up giveaways, for people undergoing treatment for any type of cancer. These workshops make people feel like themselves again, which is invaluable.

Don't forget to look out for tap donations. There are more than thirty-five contactless tap points installed across the UK's capital city! With a tap of your card you can donate £3 to 22 homelessness charities in the capital, and these clever little card scanners are also dotted around the windows of London charity shops – a quick, easy and super simple way to give! The more you tap, the more likely it is that these will be rolled out across the UK.

Fundraising
There are a million different ways to fundraise, but the main aim is to generate money through either an

organised activity or personal enterprise. The joy of fundraising is that you can do LITERALLY ANYTHING YOU WANT to raise money, and that's what activism is all about: taking one thing you're good at and one thing you care about. Barclay's Future of Giving survey recently showed that 70 per cent of charities polled see online fundraising as 'the way forward', and 50 per cent of all charities are actively exploring investment in 'new ways' for their supporters to donate.*

Maybe you're good at drawing. Why not create some original artwork and sell it for charity online or to family and friends? If you're crafty – you love ceramics or collage or sewing – you could make small, affordable trinkets, and then send a portion of the money to a great cause. If you want to push yourself, try something active and ask your family and friends to sponsor you online. To get your fundraising juices flowing, note down:

---

* The report can be found here: www.barclayscorporate.com/content/
dam/corppublic/corporate/Documents/Industry-expertise/the-future-of-
giving.pdf (accessed March 2019).

A few things you like/love doing:

1.

2.

3.

4.

5.

Any charities, causes or things you care about:

1.

2.

3.

4.

5.

Now, look back at those lists. Do any of the things have a link or similarities? For instance, if you've written down 'gardening' as something you love doing and 'climate change' as something you care about, there is nothing stopping you growing and selling plants to raise money.

To give you a hit of inspiration, let's look at some awesome people who have done just that to raise money for important causes. Study their socials, look at their websites and you'll see that they make sure the product, branding and idea all tie to one purpose. It's made clear to the buyer, which means they are likely to buy and support the cause.

Natalie Byrne
@nataliebyrne

Natalie Byrne is a Latina illustrator based in London, known for her purpose-led and educational illustrations that focus on women's issues. That's why it made perfect sense for Natalie to publish her illustrated book, *Period*, and then produce T-shirts, prints and other items from which 10 per cent of the profits go to fighting period poverty. A creative campaign that comes full circle.

Lauren Mahon
@girlvscancer

Lauren Mahon is a thirty-two-year-old breast cancer survivor and blogger. Partnering with a network of amazing women across social media, Lauren designed and created a limited edition T-shirt to raise funds and awareness of breast cancer, splitting 25 per cent of GIRLvsCANCER Tit-Tees and ALL money raised from GIRLvsCANCER events and brand collaborations equally four ways between GIRLvsCANCER partner charities. An innovative way to fundraise for a seriously important cause, with a human story at the centre and a mission that offers real value to supporters and followers.

Tori Ratcliffe
@toriratcliffeart

Tori is a friend of mine from uni, a genius artist and owner of Spud – a lovely stray puppy I brought back from Greece. Tori creates stunning animal watercolours, pet portrait commissions and homeware to raise money for conservation charities, and as it stands she has raised more than a huge £14,000! She is the perfect example of using your creative talent for good.

If you're feeling inspired but still a little stuck on what to do, I've got ya back. Here's a bunch of ideas to get your creative fundraising juices flowing:

A sponsored run, night walk, cross-country walk, hike, dance, workout or swim challenge. A ticketed book swap or clothes swap. A car boot sale or yard sale (good for the environment too!). A ticketed dinner party or cocktail party. Host a gig in your backyard with a local band. Bingo for family, or drink bingo for you and a bunch of mates. A ticketed movie night, outdoor or indoor. A raffle: brands are willing to give away products to be linked to a good cause. Adopt a viral challenge, make it harder and ask people to donate online. Babysit and give a small portion of your wage to a relevant charity. A themed bar-crawl; everyone gives a pound per bar. Board game marathon, entry-free fantasy football, two team cook-offs, a table tennis, ping pong, darts, pool or beer pong tournament. A car wash, dog walking, window cleaning, gardening; people will always pay you to do even an hour of the things they can't be bothered to do. Sky-diving, bowl-a-thon, morning yoga workshop outdoors, a workshop of any of your talents with kids, auction of designer clothes or antiques, pamper or spa day with friends, tick-eted house party, summer street party, potluck picnic, bake sale or Great British Charity Bake Off, art sale, charity BBQ, sleepover, trivia night or pub quiz, karaoke competition.

The whole point of fundraising is that you can do literally anything you want and monetise it to create funds for charity. It can be the silliest or most fun thing you can think of (bets on a drinking game, anyone?) or a serious personal challenge (someone I know *actually did* three marathons in a row) – if people are really getting something out of it they're more likely to put their hands in their pockets and support your cause. But always keep in mind that your 'action' should fit with the issue you're trying to solve. Some fundraising efforts can be tone deaf. A good rule of thumb is to ask yourself, 'Would direct survivors of this problem want to be involved in this effort?' Make it tasteful. Make it inclusive and have an honest dialogue with those you're trying to help.

Remember: When your birthday rolls around, there's a really easy opportunity to pay it forward. Facebook Birthday Fundraisers are not entirely unlike Facebook's crowdfunding element, but they specifically use your birthday as motivation for your followers to donate rather than buying you gifts. All you need to do is pick a charity and post a status asking people to give to your fundraiser instead of buying you presents – but remember to make sure your birthday is set to 'public' so that your network will automatically be prompted! Plus, if you're not a decisive person or you'd struggle to organise or work out a fundraising event, this way the decision is made for you and all the hard work done by Facebook. Cheers, Mark. You've done one thing right.

Crowdfunding online

Now, I'm guessing you know what crowdfunding is, and the good it can do for small businesses and individuals, but the amount of people using it to raise money for charity and strangers in need of help is growing exponentially. Sure, the concept of collecting small amounts of money off many people to create a large-scale life-changing amount is nothing new, but for too long the power to collect was only in institutions' hands. Now, we can raise money for whatever the hell we want with strangers from our sofa – woo hoo!

I had a particularly life-affirming experience with crowdfunding, actually. When I lived on a boat in Greece between 2015 and 2016 (long story!), a bunch of stray dogs lived on an island that we always came back to. I fell in love with a little white stray puppy and called him Spud. After three months of trying to find him a home, my friend Tori (mentioned above in reference to her excellent art) offered to foster him and we set about raising the money through Facebook, Instagram and Twitter to get him to the UK where she lived. Crowdfunding made it possible because I could raise money from people all over the world without being there, and I could access that money instantly. The possibilities are endless with crowdfunding, and as it's effectively an online fundraising format, you could also use it to raise money for causes you care about by pairing it with any of the activities in the Fundraising section above!

How to start a crowdfunding campaign

1. *Make sure it's clear and eye-catching*

Your campaign needs to be really specific and have a well-communicated clear outcome. Put some time aside to brand your landing page – wherever you host it – with a consistent look and feel, because if it's a nice place to be people will be more likely to share it on their own pages. If it's got a huge, complicated or pixelated image that doesn't quite fit, or is busy, with too many colours, texts and features on one page, people aren't going to want to spend time there or show it off. Secondly, get the important info across quickly: what is the charity, what do they do and what percentage of the donations goes towards this work? The more transparency on where someone's money is going, the more likely they are to give. As the founder of the crowdfunding page, it's up to you to make the pitch clear and concise. Tell any potential donors why you are choosing this charity and this cause. Always remember to make the time limit clear, too: detailing when your crowd-funder runs out upfront means people will be more likely not to delay donating.

2. *Set a realistic funding target*

There's no point setting a super-high target for your first crowdfunder if you haven't grown interest in the cause already. If people are coming into this cold, they're less likely to donate helpful amounts. Start with a realistic target and then you can grow interest from there because people will feel like a part of the journey. Plus, if your target is realistic people will be able to see visible momentum as donations move towards the target. Stale crowdfunders that don't look like they've got momentum are way less likely to inspire people to donate.

3. *Choose the right type of crowdfunder*
Not all crowdfunders are created equally, so here's how the main ones work:

- Regular donations: people donate to a cause asking nothing in return.
- Reward donations: people donate and you reward them with something. This could be an event, a gift – you choose. Is this something you could do, and if so, what could you offer to encourage people to donate? Think realistically here. Don't get yourself in a mess and only offer what you can.
- All or nothing: people donate, and *only if you reach the target, does the money go to the cause your designated cause.* This is when it's important to be very realistic about your target. It may seem unfair, but research suggests these are often more successful than Keep It All campaigns.
- Keep It All: people donate and even if you don't reach the target, the money goes to your cause. This is great for causes that are time-sensitive. I used a 'Keep It All' campaign to help rescue Spud from Greece, because I only had a week to

raise the money and it proved really useful – he now lives in Edinburgh and is the happiest dog in the world!

4. *Keep your donors updated*
Always remember that people are giving their hard-earned cash to this cause, so keeping them updated on the movements of your crowdfunder is the least you can do. Plus, it pushes them to share it more. Could you detail what the money they've already raised could do? Could you let them know how the subject of the crowdfunder is doing? Anything to keep your cause fresh, human and relevant will help.

5. *Have a contingency plan for extra funds*
Let donors know what you will do with the money if you raise over the target. For instance, when I ran the crowdfunder to bring Spud back from Greece, I made it super clear that any extra funds raised would go to locally run dog shelters, so that people were less inclined to hold off donating if the money was nearing its target.

THINGS TO REMEMBER IF YOU'RE CROWDFUNDING FOR SOMEONE YOU DON'T KNOW
Raising money for people we don't know has become one of the quickest and easiest ways to ease suffering we hear about online or in the news. But there are a few things to think about before you do:

1. Find the person, somehow, and get in contact with them to ensure they're happy receiving the money. Money and finances are very, very personal issues and however much you may imagine they'd love the free money, they may not. Also they might not want their story to receive more press (I say 'more' as most 'stranger-fundraisers' come from people finding someone in need through the internet or news). Be sure you have their blessing to go ahead first.

2. Ensure you tell their story responsibly. You want to get it right and not sensationalise. Personal stories are just that, personal, and you're telling a story that isn't necessarily yours to tell, so try and get them to okay your copy for the page before you send.

3. Choose a platform that means they get all the money, and make sure you know exactly how you're going to transfer it to them when you're done. Plus, if you're raising money for someone who needs whatever they can get, you're going to want to make sure you select a 'keep it all' campaign. Not reaching your target and then not being able to provide them with the money because you missed the target is the most common crowdfunding #fail.

4. Be as transparent as you can about how you will handle the money. You're not a corporation with rules and regulations, so you're going to have to work for people to trust you a little more. Be as clear and straightforward about

what the money will go towards and how you will allocate the funds, and be prepared for questions.

Remember that crowdfunding is about regular people giving money to regular people, and because of that, there aren't water-tight rules on where your money is going. Of course, we all want to see the best in people, but using one of the major platforms is a clever move as there is more protection in terms of ensuring the money is handled properly and goes where it should.

Here are a few platforms to consider:

JustGiving Campaigns
These guys allow you to have a branded page, they inform your network of any updates and they also have a functionality that allows your supporters to start splinter fundraisers for your cause. More people power means more eyes on your cause and more donations.

GoFund Me
These guys are the only major crowdfunding platform that charges absolutely nothing to set up a campaign, which is great news, plus they also have 24/7 online support for every campaigner and no penalties for missing your goal. Win, win, win.

Facebook funding
The world's biggest social platform is making crowdfunding easier than ever with the two-tap donate button and no

charity fees for all of the charities registered with Facebook. The great part is that you already have a pre-created network ready to donate, especially if it's something your family or friends have an affinity with.

THE POWER OF TIME

There's something people always underestimate the value of: time. Volunteering your time can actually be just as important, and often more meaningful than donating your money.

Educating yourself

I'm tempted to write this next sentence as bold and as big as this page because it's bloody important:

Self-education is the single most important thing you can do to challenge society.

I'll give that sentence a second to settle in. Nice.

The importance of education is drilled into us from before we can walk. Education is a huge privilege in itself, so it's rightfully forced upon those of us lucky enough to have the opportunity to learn. But there are different types of education and self-education is, I think, one of the most important. At its least it is an interesting experience, and at its most useful it can spark something big inside of us and

SELF-EDUCATION IS THE SINGLE MOST IMPORTANT THING YOU CAN DO TO CHALLENGE SOCIETY.

lead to empathy, understanding, passion or even change. Critically, it's open to absolutely everyone, too. Sure, the time needed to self-educate is definitely a luxury, but the access is there for all and that is absolutely key when it comes to levelling the playing field. When austerity means cuts to education budgets, and resources are becoming ever more stretched, we still have libraries (just), we still have books and we still have the internet. We can still learn. Plus, the information being served to us now is far less regulated. Yes, we can cherry-pick what we want to learn about and internet algorithms make it way too easy for us to stay within the small sphere of our political and moral views, but the point is, if we want to get a broad spectrum of information, we can. It's imperative that in the opinion culture we live in, we make sure that the information we're consuming is balanced. Online, we're specifically fed the idea that consuming opposing viewpoints makes us less of an authority on an issue, but I would argue the opposite. As Ryan, my lawyer, once told me when I refused to read a piece in the *Sun*, 'You have to look at other narratives even if you don't like them. Shying away from reading what you disagree with hinders you from making informed decisions as to how you can persuade, criticise or undermine.' Would I buy the *Sun* and fund their work? No. Will I read it so I understand the 'opposition'? Yes. The truth is, many of us haven't had the privilege of education throughout our lives, and the luxury of reading and learning about the world isn't possible for all, so those of us who have the opportunity must take it upon ourselves to grab it, with both hands, and do the work to understand our society and the complex problems within it – and that includes seeing different viewpoints and issues through a different lens.

The beauty of self-education is that there are no limits. You can gobble up information and facts on all sorts of issues quickly by listening to podcasts on your commute, or you can invest in one single social issue and consume reports, newspaper articles and informational texts, whatever you want to learn about – and in whatever format – the education and therefore your personal development is in your own hands.

Volunteering
The UN General Assembly defines volunteering as 'activities undertaken of free will, for the general public good and where monetary reward is not the principal motivating factor'.* Volunteering is about donating your time to better your society or community in some way, and generally you can split it up into four separate ways. Try and think of them as:

1. *Mutual aid/self-help*
Work carried out in groups by peers or people who share a problematic health, economic or social condition or situation. These groups work to alleviate or improve the

---

* 'UNGA Resolution 56/38: Recommendations on Support for Volunteering', UN Volunteers website, www.unv.org/publications/unga-resolution-5638-recommendations-support-volunteering (accessed March 2019).

circumstances of their fellow people. It's important to remember that reciprocal relationships are key to this form of volunteering – generally it's about both giving and receiving support in a safe space.

For example: being an advocate and ambassador for a mental health charity

2. *Service to others*

This one's self-explanatory, but it's about giving your time to a cause to provide immediate relief to individuals and communities, and becoming part of an initiative or activity that aims to provide support or service to people without asking anything in return. Basically, being an actively kind person.

For example: volunteering at a homeless shelter at Christmas!

3. *Civic participation*

This one sounds like jargon but stay with me. Civic participation is about offering your time to be part of the political or social systems that are responsible for policy, access to services and more. It's about using your time to engage in work that may not provide immediate relief or support to people, but works towards making politics, policies or systems that affect people's lives better in the long run.

For example: volunteering to do admin or research for a local MP.

4. *Advocacy and campaigning*
This is one of the most common, especially online. It's about donating your time to raise awareness of, and get people on board with, an issue. Then using that advocacy to push for change, either with a group or alone, on an issue you're passionate about.

For example: volunteering to canvass for an electoral campaign or campaigning against a community issue e.g. fracking.

Now we've got the basics down, answer these three questions to help you work out what you give a damn about and what kind of volunteering you'd enjoy, and remember that volunteering isn't always one-sided, but can be great for learning new skills or developing existing ones.

1. *What do you enjoy doing? (This could be organising, painting or physically pushing yourself – anything!)*

2. *What community, team or work skills are you good at?*

3. *What community, team or work skills do you want to be better at?*

Think about your answers and note down as many extras as you can. Think outside what you like doing now, but also what you liked or were good at doing as a kid, too. Do you think often about women's rights, animal rights, or youth violence, or did you care a huge amount about conservation when you were little? Let's say it's conservation: have you thought about volunteering to plant trees for a weekend, or propagating at a local flower nursery? Let's say you want to improve your writing, or you're good at using social platforms. Could you lend design skills or copywriting skills, or even social media skills, to a small initiative run in your community with a poor online presence? Could you flyer for events that are doing good for the community? Spend a couple of hours at the local dog shelter? Become a weekly companion for an elderly person? To work out what kinds of volunteering opportunities are near you, head to do-it.org or reachvolunteering.org.uk and get stuck in.

Volunteering is something that's desperately needed in any and every community. Large charities like Age UK, Barnardo's, British Red Cross, Cancer Research UK, the National Trust and The Prince's Trust are always looking for people, but they also have a huge reach so they have more chance of finding volunteers. Hunt out smaller, independent initiatives that need help online – they're more likely to be flexible, too. For example, a wonderful friend of mine recently began volunteering for anti-period poverty charity Bloody Good Period. She goes for a couple of hours every now and then, so it fits around her job easily, plus she's learning new skills, meeting new people and making new connections. This gives her a real sense of purpose. Plus, the opportunity to get real-world experience is also brilliant. You can always look at activism as an opportunity for yourself, too; being a volunteer means getting the opportunity to learn about a different industry or world. For example, I always wanted to work in marine biology, but was I academic enough? No way. I scraped a pass in my science exams even with paid-for extra help, and I just naturally really struggled to retain that kind of information, so it was clear I wasn't going to be able to complete the years of further science education needed. With volunteering, I could help with marine conservation research, collect data on species or be cleaning baby turtles if I really wanted to. You can get a taste of any industry by volunteering while providing them with an extra pair of hands, so it really is a win-win.

Acts of kindness
One of the easiest ways to volunteer your time is to consider incorporating acts of kindness into your day-to-day life. Here are some ideas of how to really make a difference to someone's day:

- Take the bins out for an elderly person who lives nearby
- Buy a coffee for the person behind you in the line at your local cafe
- Swap Starbucks for your local cafe
- Use a reusable coffee cup instead of the disposable ones
- Leave notes of encouragement on the windscreens of cars
- Plant a tree for the environment

- Buy some treats for your office
- Send the hair from your haircut to a donation centre
- Mentor a young child over email
- Donate money to a local charity on Random Acts of Kindness Day (17 February)
- Give up your seat for someone else even if they didn't ask
- Leave a pound in a shopping trolley at your local supermarket
- Leave great books you've read in quiet spots
- Spend five minutes picking up litter on your walk home
- Tell someone if you think they look lovely, or you love their outfit
- Tip more than you should
- Let others go in line in front of you
- Write a positive review (we are so quick to write bad ones!)

Remember: We are all so unused to others being kind to us and asking for nothing in return that people may be shocked or not give you the reaction you want. That's okay, and a great tip is to make what you're doing clear: 'I'm trying to be kinder in my day-to-day life, so thought I'd [fill in].'

THE POWER OF NUMBERS

A lot of pushing for change is about raising awareness. It's about showing people why something is important or needs to change, and then presenting that argument to the people who can help you make that change. Regardless of the issue you're trying to solve, whether big or small, illustrating that it affects multiple people – not just you or your community – can be pretty powerful. It's hard to ignore an issue when thousands of people are asking you to do something about it.

Petitions

A petition is a really easy way to show your support. Petitions have got a bad name in the press in recent years because of their link with 'one-click activism', but at the end of the day, putting your name to something you care about is a single act that could really help someone change something. Signing a petition is in itself a micro-act of change, but it would be very easy to sit at your laptop and sign one for every headline you see that pulls at your heartstrings. Although there's nothing inherently wrong with that (at all), it serves as a reminder of how easy it is to support a hundred things quickly, and not a few things well. We all only have limited time in the day, so if you want to make a good contribution to someone's fight, quickly google the petition you're about to sign and any core information you find in the petition info box.

That way, you'll be able to see if the petition is part of a bigger campaign or fight, and you may be able to help in other ways or get involved. At the time of writing, 111,098 people have signed my petition and I'm sure a lot of them have forgotten they had even done it. However, I did get messaged on Facebook by a couple of people who had signed it and wanted to do more. One woman pointed me in the direction of some charities who helped me get a little press at the beginning, and another woman owned an online community where she shared the petition. When I was trying to find victims' stories later on, she put a call-out on her community and it helped me get my first stats on upskirting. The point is, any connection made can be helpful to the petition creator so remember, your involvement doesn't have to finish with your signature.

Marches and rallies

Rallies and marches are one of the oldest and most easily recognised examples of activism, which is why they have been used in activism iconography and are the visuals most used to represent a revolution. They seem to be, by nature, quite reactionary but often they are part of a larger strategy.

A rally is a demonstration or a protest for or against a given cause by a group of people. Its main objective is to cause disruption in some way and bring attention to an issue. Marches, by contrast, are generally a more peaceful and methodical way to protest. Both can be super effective when it comes to acting as a catalyst for progress, but choosing when and where to have them is absolutely critical. For example, if we're talking about a large-scale issue that affects entire societies, rallies can be very effective – mostly because they raise awareness of an issue and put public pressure on institutions. Think of the large-scale organised climate change rallies and marches, for example, that have become more and more common in central London; they put clear and continual pressure on policymakers and show that the public are not letting an issue lie, regardless of how much time passes. They act as a constant reminder to those in power that people want change.

Now, let's take my campaign. There were periods of time – actually months at a time – when the politicians we were dealing with weren't engaging with us or listening to us in the way we'd hoped, so we had to put the pressure on in some way, and make them realise we were still there and weren't going away. If I had organised a rally or a march during the frustrating and quiet periods of my campaign, it would have done me a huge disservice. In fact, some individuals and media companies were recommending that I, and often trying to force me to, organise a march. They told me it would be a great news story and would put huge pressure on the government, but I made a decision – one I made multiple times during my work – to put the campaign ahead of the media. I realised a rally would only have made me less trustworthy in the eyes of the very people I wanted to work with; the very people who had the power to change the law. They would have seen it as showmanship over hard graft. For me, it was entirely a last resort, one I hoped I'd never have to turn to, because I didn't need a 'fist in the air' ostentatious fight. I needed to work hard behind the scenes with the people in power and gain their trust. As a general rule of thumb, when it comes to your own work, you need to decide whether demonstrations will actually help progress the trajectory of your work, or whether they will do it damage. For broader issues like Brexit and climate change, issues that affect huge groups of people but that you are not necessarily an authority on, marches and rallies can be incredibly effective, whereas for more niche and personal issues they may not be.

Voting

In the words of Gloria Steinem, 'Voting is not the most we can do. But it is the least.' If you can afford not to vote, then you should be voting. Democracy is, I believe, a privilege, and we all have a duty to be active in asking for what we want from our society. Now, I can't tell you how to vote because, well, that wouldn't be democracy, but here I'll break down elections and how to register:

Local elections
For some reason, everyone tends to get excited about the general elections but not the local elections – what! They are just as important! Local elections are held in different parts of the country, and are usually held around every four years. They give you the opportunity to elect

representatives for your local council, but guess what, these are the people who will go into Parliament and may have the power to make decisions about your society, so choose wisely. Effectively, you are given an opportunity to vote people into that space. Unlike a general election, this is a great opportunity for communities to help diversify their governing body and vote individuals in who actually represent their local areas.*

General elections

A general election must be held every five years and a new Parliament is elected. Effectively every seat in the House becomes 'vacant' and each constituency has the opportunity to vote for the person they want to represent them in the House of Commons. Generally, there's a handful of MPs standing for each constituency. Usually, the political party that wins the most seats in the House (which comes from your votes) forms the government.†

How to register

This sounds like one of the most boring things you'll ever be asked to do, but it literally takes less time than it does to drink a glass of wine. First things first, you do not need to register separately for every election. You only need to register again if you've changed address, name or nationality.

---

* For further information, visit www.gov.uk/elections-in-the-uk/local-government (accessed March 2019).

† For further information, visit www.parliament.uk/about/how/elections-and-voting/general (accessed March 2019).

Here's how to register:

- Grab your passport and your NI number
- Head to registertovote.service.gov.uk
- Fill out the form
- Wow, you're so politically engaged!

Voting

Voting can be hard and confusing sometimes, because often we may not feel like everyone's policies or manifestos reflect our views. Read a party's manifesto from a few different sites to get a more non-biased overview first, and then vote for who best represents how you feel on a fundamental level. Whose views most closely reflect yours out of everyone? Remember though, you're not voting for yourself here. You're voting for those who can't and you're voting to make everyone's lives better, not just your own.

If there's one thing you take from this book, make it acting on one of the sections in this chapter. Do something small, and see how you feel. Activism is never an entirely altruistic endeavour, and there's no harm in doing something that makes you feel good if it's good for others too. So sign that petition or volunteer for half a day! Whatever form of people power you choose, you just need to remember it is power. It may feel small, but small acts of change make movements. A bee is just an annoying bee, but a swarm? That's some powerful shit.

4

WHITE PRIVILEGE
AND ACTIVISM

❝ *The only way we do away with white
supremacy is when white people decide it's
time to do the work.*❞

Aja Barber

B efore I start this chapter, I want you to know that these are
my personal thoughts on white privilege and how it intersects
with activism. This chapter is also mostly helpful to those who hold
significant privilege, and particularly white privilege. I realise this
chapter won't be for everybody and their specific privileges, but from
where I stand, it feels like an important addition to this book. It
is key to be transparent about where I'm at, and, to hammer this
home, I've invited someone I respect to help with this chapter. Aja

Barber is a writer, fashion consultant and anti-racism educator. In this chapter, which was written by me in one go and is unedited, I have asked Aja to make any notes or amendments and to draw my attention to my shortcomings. The purpose of this is to show those of you who hold privilege reading this that you're going to be wrong sometimes, you're going to fuck up, you're going to be held accountable for it at times, and that's okay. It's more than okay – it's good. First, we'll start with my unedited version:

MY EXPERIENCE WITH WHITE PRIVILEGE

If someone told me changing the law had a lot to do with luck, my immediate reaction would be to become defensive and tell them 'how hard' I've worked. I'd initially want to correct them, to tell them that everything that happened to me was down to my own graft; the 5am rises, the thousands of emails. But, the truth is, it wasn't. I have had a lot of help.

- I am white
- I am slim
- I am young
- I am heterosexual
- I am non-disabled
- I am cis-gendered (the gender I identify with matches my sex)
- I was born into a world above the poverty line
- I come from a family which hasn't struggled with mental illness

- I come from a supporting, loving family environment
- I live in London
- The list goes on.
- (And on. And on.)

From this list you can see that I have a whole host of unearned benefits in my life. These, my friends, are called *privileges*. And if you've never thought about having privilege, that means you definitely *do*; you have the privilege of being totally unaware of your privilege. To illustrate how privilege works, let's think of a super high wall that you're trying to climb over. On the other side of the wall is what you want to achieve – for me, that was the law change. Around you there are multiple people from different backgrounds standing at the base of their own walls, ready to climb. Now, for every fact in the above list, take a row of bricks off the height of my wall. Give me fewer to climb; to fight against. The bricks removed illustrate the obstacles removed from my path, and show you how each fact about my identity benefits me and makes my task easier. Suddenly, getting over that wall is looking a lot more likely for me.

If you've been privy to any conversations on equality (and if not, wow, are you in deep now) you will have heard the word 'meritocracy'. White people, specifically, love to talk about 'meritocracy'. Maybe during these conversations you've heard people retort that someone 'got paid more because he had more experience', or that someone 'was hired because they were the best person for the job'.

Although this may seem a fair assessment when talking about a singular situation – and although it may be true in some cases – it's critical to remember that our society, and specifically the way our institutions are run, and jobs are landed, has never been a meritocracy. People don't get opportunities based solely on merit when the game has always been rigged in one group of people's favour. White people have always had more opportunity, more chances, more stability and more support. The fact that that 'hot white male actor' is being paid more than the 'hot white female actor' opposite him in a TV show isn't 'fair' because he had more roles and was more well-known than her. He had more roles and was more well-known because he is a 'hot white male actor', and a 'hot white male actor' has, historically, always landed the roles. As I said, rigged system.

When it comes to activism, simply having the ability to choose whether you engage with it is a privilege. Many people don't get to choose. They have to. At the beginning of the campaign, when I was trying to gain some media attention so I could get signatures for my petition, I knew that being a slim, young white woman would mean newspapers and websites would put me in their articles, that they would use pictures of me in their pieces. After all, that's what they do. They would love the story of the poor, young upskirting victim fighting back. But would the coverage of my campaign have been the same had I been a black woman from below the poverty line? Would the way they framed me and my story be the same if I was a disabled person? Would the words that surrounded my photo have had the same supportive narrative and unequivocal faith in me succeeding? I don't think so.

My whiteness, among other things, benefited me because we prioritise whiteness. White is the main power source. White is the default. Our industries are owned by white people. Our country is run by white people. Our media showcases white people. White people prioritise white people. So, when I stepped into media studios or into Parliament, society was expecting to see me. I wasn't an 'anomaly' to them, and therefore, I wasn't treated as one. This is white privilege. Sure, it doesn't mean I didn't work hard, but it does mean that I didn't have to work *harder* because of the colour of my skin. It means that the way I look didn't hinder me each step of the way. It means a ridiculous amount of obstacles were removed for me, because I'm a 'Natural Beige' in foundation. This, for me, is the main privilege I need to be aware of. It is the most damaging. You, on the other hand, may be benefiting from a different type of privilege – financial privilege, thin privilege, or many privileges combined, like me. But for now, let's focus on white privilege. It's important to note here that I'm aware I've spoken about gender bias in the media, and that's because it's the *one* thing that society has over me. Men are the only oppressive force in my life, so I've spoken about how I had to work harder as a young woman in male-dominated spaces, because I've been asked about it more times than I can count. The thing is, I've *never* been asked about the things I didn't have to work harder because of. Not once have I been asked about my privilege. Because no one wants to discuss it. Because discussing it would imply that there's an opposite to privilege, and people don't want to face up to that.

Here are three things to do with your privilege, written and explained by people of colour:

RECOGNISE IT

❝ The idea of white privilege forces white people who aren't actively racist to confront their own complicity in its continuing existence. White privilege is dull, grinding complacency. It is par for the course in a world in which drastic race inequality is responded to with a shoulder shrug, considered just the norm.❞

Reni Eddo Lodge,
Why I'm No Longer Talking To White People About Race

CHECK IT

❝ When somebody asks you to "check your privilege" they are asking you to pause and consider how the advantages you've had in life are contributing to your opinions and *actions, and how the lack of disadvantages in certain areas is keeping you from fully understanding the struggles others are facing and may in fact be contributing to those struggles.*

Ijeoma Oluo,
So You Want To Talk About Race

USE IT

Claiming you aren't racist is meaningless; what matters is recognizing racism, calling it by its name, and working to eradicate it. A person who complains about their privilege is like a lottery winner grumbling about the burdens of money to someone making minimum wage [...] "If I had white privilege, I don't think I'd be ashamed of it," I wrote. "I'd use it to expose injustice and work to make things better."

Renée Graham,
'Use Your White Privilege to Fight Racism'*

---

* Renée Graham, 'Use Your White Privilege to Fight Racism', *Boston Globe*, 24 April 2018, www.bostonglobe.com/opinion/2018/04/24/use-your-white-privilege-fight-racism/l3kE21EFsMpTF6uboe72pI/story.html.

Distilled down, activism should be an empowering space for everyone. It has to be otherwise it isn't valuable. I've already called it a democratic buffet, but the truth is, it still suffers from the biases that come with class, privilege and racism, because it works within, and alongside, institutions that prioritise whiteness and therefore benefit from racism. I will hold my hands up and say I have worked with and inside structures that are built on racism. I've been part of those structures and I've done it in my activism because I had to, to force change. I have to be close to some structures to hold them accountable and have conversations, but I draw the line at aiding them if they have no interest in developing for the better. The truth is definitely that up until I started this work, I have not understood fully what's needed of me to counter and help deconstruct those structures and the danger caused by white privilege. We should all admit that, too. Because admitting is the first step towards deconstructing, thinking critically and unlearning – something we all need to do.

Finally, here are a few things that are important to consider when going into activism:

1. *Is this your story to tell?*
It is critical that we learn about, become passionate about, and raise awareness of issues that don't directly affect us. However, supporting and stealing are two very different things, and there is one stage of activism where it's especially key to check and be aware of your privilege: when choosing what you want to work on. Far, far too often, we

see people telling stories that aren't theirs. We often see individuals using knowledge they have learned from others to gain recognition. We see stories that don't belong to them, that could be told better by someone else, coming out of their mouths. This is because as privileged people, we are entirely used to having our opinions and our stories listened to. We've never had to fight to be heard, so we feel entitled to be the voice for everything, but every story isn't ours to tell; a man starting a campaign about what it's like to be a woman and paid less than a man in the same job would be laughed out of the room. Equally, if you have no experience of FGM, the culture around it, the narrative or the root cause of it, you have no place to be an authority on it. Even if you care about it and want to help.

The most important thing you can do as a privileged person is give others a platform to speak about issues that you have no lived experience of.

Want to give money, resources and time to a cause you don't have experience of? Amazing! Do it! That's support! Want to make it your thing and tell everyone about it? Think again. Try empowering others to tell their story instead of telling it for them. It's important to flag this, for everyone, because when a story *is* told by the right person, and when a passion is pursued by someone who truly understands it – who lives it – only then can the work be honest, good work. When change comes from someone who needs to make it, their heart is in the right place and they're much more likely to get people on board. When a story is theirs to tell, the solution is better for everyone. We don't need to take issues from those who know more about them and act as if we can solve them. The world doesn't need white saviours, it needs white allies.

2. *Listen*

A lot of the time activism can feel like it's all about getting your point across. You'll need to convince people of your cause often, and you'll have many, many conversations, at length, about your work. You will want to argue your point and – if you do the work for long enough – people will treat you as an authority, and ask you for answers. However, not letting this become your default position is absolutely critical, because the most important moments will come when you *listen*. As a person with privilege, we are naturally used to having an answer to everything (my dad could tell you this about me at *length*), but an incredibly important part of being privileged is remembering that you don't know everything about everyone. You don't have all the answers, and you only know about life when it pertains to your personal experience. Everything else is to be learned about, and you'll learn it from others. Now, this may sound like obvious stuff, but it isn't. Those with significant privilege – especially white people – are great at caring about and opening up about their own personal life and problems, and terrible at being generally interested in – and listening to – different experiences, and must get better at that and lead by example. Your work is never done if you're privileged, and because of that, your work is never done as an activist. So, when it comes to people from different backgrounds, with different experiences and especially from marginalised communities, your job is not to talk, but to listen. Then help them get their voice and experiences heard. Pass the mic.

3. *Diversify your feed and your life*
Until October 2016, Elon Musk didn't follow a single woman on Twitter. Then a website called him out on it, so he hastily clicked the blue button on a handful of women he knew of. Don't be like Elon. Pick up your phone right now and open the platform you spend the most time on. Are you an Instagram obsessive, or do you love getting your point across quickly via Twitter? Regardless, I can almost guarantee that if you're white, your feed is filled with people who look like you. And when you're consuming information, opinion and stories from people just like you, it's guaranteed that you'll become so accustomed to your own life experiences that you'll fail to understand and acknowledge your own inherent biased perspective. This is called being blinded by your privilege, and it only allows your work to be at best limited, and at worst damaging, as it'll perpetuate the prioritisation of white people above all others. It's not enough to 'be aware' of people of colour. We need to be listening and learning. You can head to www. diversifyyourfeed.org to check the gender (im)balance of your Twitter feed, but when it comes to ensuring you have

a mix of people from different backgrounds and walks of life, that's down to each of us individually.

To start off, make sure you:

- Consider all forms of diversity: this is not just about following more women, and it's definitely not about following more women that look and sound like you. This is about race, ethnicity, gender, economic background, age, physical abilities, political beliefs and more.
- Use a 'web' effect when searching out people to follow. Search the people you know of from different backgrounds and look at who they are platforming, retweeting and communicating with.
- Don't just add people who are different to you and go back to scrolling through the same accounts: listen to them. This is not about performative wokeness. It's about actually making an effort to read, listen to and understand people with different stories from you. The great thing is the more you do that, the more of it you'll be served by the algorithm.
- Don't let it finish there. It's important to understand that allowing someone else to educate you almost entirely is not great. I know that, as a woman, I sometimes feel sort of exhausted having to consistently explain, discuss or call out stuff with the men in my life. I'm so happy to do it because I am positive it helps, but that information should

act as a starting point rather than a full-time job. So, remember to take the basic understanding you've gained from someone on certain topics and begin proactively self-educating from there.

- Look around at the people you surround yourself with in real life: do they all look like you? Do they come from similar backgrounds? Do they have the same lifestyle as you? If so, you're likely to only really understand the 'type' of experiences and problems those like you have. Ensure you're making an effort to diversify what you're consuming through your screens and take the opportunity to listen to and learn from people unlike you in real life when you can.

4. *Pay it back*

The truth is, we're in a funny place when it comes to paying people back for their activism and emotional labour (see: teaching and educating you on their experience for free). Brands are more than happy to work with people like me because my work and identity happen to fit into the commercialisation of 'modern feminism', which is proving pretty lucrative for them. You'd be forgiven for thinking that brands want to be associated with women constantly at the moment, but not all womxn. They're often really not that inclusive. They are less likely to work with the LGBTQIA+ community and women of colour because many individuals from those communities are – quite rightly – very vocal about the discrimination and oppression they experience.

They call out inequality and are critical of society, and for some reason brands are still distancing themselves from that bravery and honesty. I know so many incredible people who are educating others daily, but strangely, big brands don't offer them the same sort of jobs that they're offering a white woman who wears a 'This Is What A Feminist Looks Like' T-shirt made by modern slave labour, because so many brands still don't see anyone outside this very narrow archetype as valuable. To them, anyone outside that archetype won't make them money because they still see the consumer landscape as like them: a white upper-class or middle-class institution – and they can't grasp themes they haven't experienced. This is insidious racism and homophobia – the idea that different experiences don't matter in the grand scheme of things. That's why it's our job to remunerate the people we learn from. With brands only platforming and paying certain types of people, we need to make a tangible effort to support those who don't benefit from privilege. Many of the womxn we learn from on our social platforms are trying to educate us by putting out carefully crafted content and basically giving away a whole load of emotional labour and education for free. If we really care about women, shouldn't we give back, especially at a time when so many big brands aren't? If you can afford to, reach out to your favourite educators and ask if they have somewhere you can 'pay it back'. They may have a Patreon account that you can give to, or they may launch crowdfunding campaigns for projects they're working on. Keep an eye out and if you feel their work is valuable, show them the value of it.

If you fancy doing some essential legwork in this area, I suggest you put down my book right now and go and read Reni Eddo Lodge's *Why I'm No Longer Talking To White People About Race*. Go! Right now! Devour every page and spend some time filling in her Privilege Checklist. That way, you'll be able to see the things that have given you a leg up in life on a very obvious level, and the things that haven't been an obstacle for you, and don't stop there. Dive head first into educating yourself on your privilege and you'll be a better person and better activist for it.

LEARN FROM MY MISTAKES

Here, you'll find this chapter now edited by Aja Barber. Read through, look at the changes she's made, think about them and learn from my mistakes.

MY EXPERIENCE WITH WHITE PRIVILEGE

If someone told me changing the law had a lot to do with luck (and privilege), my immediate reaction would be to become defensive and tell them 'how hard' I've worked. I'd initially want to correct them, to tell them that everything that happened to me was down to my own graft; the 5am rises, the thousands of emails. But, the truth is, it wasn't. I have had a lot of help.

- I am white
- I am slim
- I am young
- You are pretty (I'm not just saying that because I'm your friend but also because being aesthetically pleasing to a dominant culture plays a huge part in this, but also you are pretty ... now I'm saying it as your friend)
- I am heterosexual
- I am non-disabled (able bodied)
- I am cis-gendered (the gender I identify with matches my sex)
- I was born into a world above the poverty line
- I come from a family which hasn't struggled with mental illness
- I come from a supporting, loving family environment
- You grew up in a two-parent home and both parents are still together (so are mine, yay!)
- I live in London (we live in one of the world's most powerful cities)
- The list goes on.
- (And on. And on.)

From this list you can see that I have a whole host of unearned benefits in my life. These, my friends, are called *privileges*. And if you've never thought about having privilege, that means you definitely *do*; you have the privilege of being totally unaware of your privilege. To illustrate how privilege works, let's think of a super high wall that you're trying to climb over. On the other side of the wall is what you want to achieve – for me, that was the law change. Around you there are multiple people from different backgrounds standing at the base of their own walls, ready to climb. Now, for every fact in the above list, take a row of bricks off the height of my wall. Give me fewer to climb; to fight against. The bricks removed illustrate the obstacles removed from my path, and show you how each fact about my identity benefits me and makes my task easier. Suddenly, getting over that wall is looking a lot more likely for me.

If you've been privy to any conversations on equality or equity (and if not, wow, are you in deep now) you will have heard the word 'meritocracy'. White people, specifically, love to talk about 'meritocracy'. Maybe during these conversations you've heard people retort that someone 'got paid more because he had more experience', or that someone 'was hired because they were the best person for the job'. Although this may seem a fair assessment when talking about a singular situation – and although it may be true in some cases – it's critical to remember that our society, and specifically the way our institutions are run, and jobs are landed, has never been a meritocracy. People don't get opportunities based solely on merit when the game has always been rigged in one group of people's favour. White people have always had more opportunity, more chances, more stability and more support. The fact that that 'hot white male actor' is being paid more than the 'hot white female actor' opposite him in a TV show isn't 'fair' because he had more roles and was more well-known than her. He had more roles and was more well-known because he is a 'hot white male actor', and a 'hot white male actor' has, historically, always landed the roles. As I said, rigged system.

When it comes to activism, simply having the ability to choose whether you engage with it is a privilege. Many people don't get to choose. They have to. People who feel they must engage do so because the inequality directly impacts their lives in ways they cannot ignore. At the beginning of the campaign, when I was trying to gain some media attention so I could get signatures for my petition, I knew that being a slim, young white woman would mean newspapers and websites would put me in their articles, that they would use pictures of me in their pieces. After all, that's what they do. They would love the story of the poor, young upskirting victim fighting back. But would the coverage of my campaign have been the same had I been a black woman from below the poverty line? Imagine how this story would play out if you were a sex worker or a transwoman. Would the way they framed me and my story be the same if I was a disabled person? Would the words that surrounded my photo have had the same supportive narrative and unequivocal faith in me succeeding? I don't think so.

My whiteness, among other things, benefited me because we prioritise whiteness. White is the main power source. White is the default. Our industries are owned by white people. Our country is run by white people. Our media showcases white people. White people prioritise white people. So, when I stepped into media studios or into Parliament, society was expecting to see me. I wasn't an 'anomaly' to them, and therefore, I wasn't treated as one. This is white privilege. Sure, it doesn't mean I didn't work hard, but it does mean that I didn't have to work *harder* because of the colour of my skin. It means that the way I look didn't hinder me each step of the way. It means a ridiculous amount of obstacles were removed for me, because I'm a 'Natural Beige' in foundation. This, for me, is the main privilege I need to be aware of. It is the most damaging. You, on the other hand, may be benefiting from a different type of privilege – financial privilege, thin privilege, or many privileges combined, like me. But for now, let's focus on white privilege. It's important to note here that I'm aware I've spoken about gender bias in the media, and that's because it's the *one* thing that society has over me. Men are the only oppressive force in my life, so I've spoken about how I had to work harder as a young woman in male-dominated spaces, because I've been asked about it more times than I can count. The thing is, I've *never* been asked about the things I didn't have to work harder because of. Not once have I been asked about my privilege. Because no one wants to discuss it. Because discussing it would infer that there's an opposite to privilege, and people don't want to face up to that.

Here are three things to do with your privilege, written and explained by people of colour:

RECOGNISE IT

❝ The idea of white privilege forces white people who aren't actively racist to confront their own complicity in its continuing existence. White privilege is dull, grinding complacency. It is par for the course in a world in which drastic race inequality is responded to with a shoulder shrug, considered just the norm. ❞

Reni Eddo Lodge, *Why I'm No Longer Talking To White People About Race*

CHECK IT

❝ When somebody asks you to "check your privilege" they are asking you to pause and consider how the advantages you've had in life are contributing to your opinions and actions, and how the lack of disadvantages in certain areas is keeping you from fully understanding the struggles others are facing and may in fact be contributing to those struggles. ❞

Ijeoma Oluo, *So You Want To Talk About Race*

USE IT

> ❛ Claiming you aren't racist is meaningless;
> what matters is recognizing racism, calling
> it by its name, and working to eradicate it. A
> person who complains about their privilege
> is like a lottery winner grumbling about
> the burdens of money to someone making
> minimum wage [...] "If I had white privilege, I
> don't think I'd be ashamed of it," I wrote. "I'd
> use it to expose injustice and work to make
> things better."❜

Renée Graham,
'Use Your White Privilege to Fight Racism'*

Distilled down, activism should be an empowering space
for everyone but until we get to that point, we have work to do.
All of us. It has to be otherwise it isn't valuable. I've already
called it a democratic buffet, but the truth is, it still suffers
from the biases that come with class, privilege and racism,
because it works within, and alongside, institutions that
prioritise whiteness and therefore benefit from racism. I
will hold my hands up and say I have worked with and

---

* Renee Graham, 'Use Your White Privilege to Fight Racism', *Boston Globe*,
24 April 2018, www.bostonglobe.com/opinion/2018/04/24/use-your-white-
privilege-fight-racism/l3kE21EFsMpTF6uboe72pI/story.html.

inside structures that are built on racism. I've been part of those structures and I've done it in my activism because I had to, to force change. Most of us are unwittingly aiding in the oppression of someone else and that is why we are having these conversations. Now is as good a time as ever. I have to be close to some structures to hold them accountable and have conversations, but I draw the line at aiding them if they have no interest in developing for the better. The truth is definitely that up until I started this work, I have not understood fully what's needed of me to counter and help deconstruct those structures and the danger caused by white privilege. We should all admit that, too. Because admitting is the first step towards deconstructing, thinking critically and unlearning – something we all need to do. ' The first thing I do in discussions about white privilege is speak about the other privileges that I have.

Finally, here are a few things that are important to consider when going into activism:

1. *Is this your story to tell?*
It is critical that we learn about, become passionate about, and raise awareness of issues that don't directly affect us. (But we have to be sure that we are ALWAYS uplifting the voices of those with less privilege than us instead of talking over them. Sharing the mic is of utmost importance.) However, supporting and stealing are two very different things, and there is one stage of activism where it's especially key to check and be aware of your privilege: when choosing what you want to work on. Far, far too often, we see people telling stories

that aren't theirs (yes, we are on the same page here). We often see individuals using knowledge they have learned from others to gain recognition. We see stories that don't belong to them, that could be told better by someone else, coming out of their mouths. (Hollywood, are you listening?) This is because as privileged people, we are entirely used to having our opinions and our stories listened to. We've never had to fight to be heard, so we feel entitled to be the voice for everything (and that entitlement extends to putting your voice in spaces where it doesn't always belong), but every story isn't ours to tell; a man starting a campaign about what it's like to be a woman and paid less than a man in the same job would be laughed out of the room (actually there was an all-male panel in New Jersey, 2017, about women's empowerment). Equally, if you have no experience of FGM, the culture around it, the narrative or the root cause of it, you have no place to be an authority on it. Even if you care about it and want to help.

The most important thing you can do as a privileged person is give others a platform to speak about issues that you have no lived experience of.

Want to give money, resources and time to a cause you don't have experience of? Amazing! Do it! That's support! Want to make it your thing and tell everyone about it? Think again. Try empowering others to tell their story instead of telling it for them. (You can even tell people within your circles about voices they should pay attention to, that's how you uplift others.) It's important to flag this, for everyone, because when a story *is* told by the right person, and when a passion is pursued by someone who truly understands it – who lives it – only then can the work be honest, good work. When change comes from someone who needs to make it, their heart is in the right place and they're much more likely to get people on board. When a story is theirs to tell, the solution is better for everyone (because authenticity matters here as well). We don't need to take issues from those who know more about them and act as if we can solve them. The world doesn't need white saviours, it needs white allies (I even say 'accomplices' – makes you sound sneaky like a spy. But also remember that ally should be a verb and not a noun. We should all be constantly learning and growing and that means that your work as an ally is never really completed. It's that old chestnut about showing your work. None of us should ever feel comfortable resting on our laurels and declaring ourselves an 'ally'. There is no need for the declaration if the work is being done.)

2. *Listen*

A lot of the time activism can feel like it's all about getting your point across. You'll need to convince people of your cause often, and you'll have many, many conversations, at length, about your work. You will want to argue your point and – if you do the work for long enough – people will treat you as an authority, and ask you for answers. However, not letting this become your default position is absolutely critical, because the most important moments will come when you *listen*. As a person with privilege, we are naturally used to having an answer to everything (my dad could tell you this about me at *length*), but an incredibly important part of being privileged is remembering that you don't know everything about everyone. You don't have all the answers, and you only know about life when it pertains to your personal experience. Everything else is to be learned about, and you'll learn it from others. Now, this may sound like obvious stuff, but it isn't. Those with significant privilege – especially white people – are great at caring about and opening up about their own personal life and problems, and terrible at being generally interested in – and listening to – different experiences, and must get better at that and lead by example. Your work is never done if you're privileged, and because of that, your work is never done as an activist. So, when it comes to people from different backgrounds, with different experiences and especially from marginalised communities, your job is not to talk, but to listen. Then help them get their voice and experiences heard. Pass the mic.

3. *Diversify your feed and your life*
Until October 2016, Elon Musk didn't follow a single woman on Twitter (I got about fifty things I could say about that and none of them are good). Then a website called him out on it, so he hastily clicked the blue button on a handful of women he knew of. Don't be like Elon. Pick up your phone right now and open the platform you spend the most

time on. Are you an Instagram obsessive, or do you love getting your point across quickly via Twitter? Regardless, I can almost guarantee that if you're white, your feed is filled with people who look like you (I see this a lot. White people want to know how to create change but some don't realise you can't get there if your feed is only filled with fellow white people). And when you're consuming information, opinion and stories from people just like you, it's guaranteed that you'll become so accustomed to your own life experiences that you'll fail to understand and acknowledge your own inherent biased perspective. This is called being blinded by your privilege, and it only allows your work to be at best limited, and at worst damaging, as it'll perpetuate the prioritisation of white people above all others. It's not enough to 'be aware' of people of colour. We need to be listening and learning (and also paying for those resources in order to bridge the gap in financial inequality). You can head to www. diversifyyourfeed.org to check the gender (im)balance of your Twitter feed (and don't forget about non-binary people), but when it comes to ensuring you have a mix of people from different backgrounds and walks of life, that's down to each of us individually.

To start off, make sure you:

- Consider all forms of diversity: this is not just about following more women, and it's definitely not about following more women that look and sound like you. This is about race, ethnicity, gender, economic background, age, physical

abilities (ability), **political beliefs** (I'm going to fight you on this one. There are several political beliefs that exist which serve to limit and oppress the movements of others. I refuse to follow those people because their views are literally hurting other humans and I can't with that. I truly believe only white people have the luxury of listening to 'both sides' because to some of us, those words are pretty violent) **and more.**

- Use a 'web' effect when searching out people to follow. Search the people you know of from different backgrounds and look at who they are platforming, retweeting and communicating with.
- Don't just add people who are different to you and go back to scrolling through the same accounts: listen to them. This is not about performative wokeness. It's about actually making an effort to read, listen to and understand people with different stories from you. The great thing is the more you do that, the more of it you'll be served by the algorithm. I tell new folks to my platform to spend the first two weeks listening before you comment. It's a rule I practice myself and it allows me to feel out the mood of a new person's space so that I'm not being disrespectful in any way when I do finally comment. It's a great way to avoid possibly putting your foot in your mouth.
- Don't let it finish there. It's important to understand that allowing someone else to

educate you almost entirely is not great. I know that, as a woman, I sometimes feel sort of exhausted having to consistently explain, discuss or call out stuff with the men in my life. I'm so happy to do it because I am positive it helps, but that information should act as a starting point rather than a full-time job. So, remember to take the basic understanding you've gained from someone on certain topics and begin proactively self-educating from there. Never expect folks to teach you every little thing. It's important to pick up some books and really dive into the work. Living within the confines of oppression is hard enough without dealing with every person who demands that you educate them when they decide it's necessary.

- Look around at the people you surround yourself with in real life: do they all look like you? Do they come from similar backgrounds? Do they have the same lifestyle as you? If so, you're likely to only really understand the 'type' of experiences and problems those like you have. Ensure you're making an effort to diversify what you're consuming through your screens and take the opportunity to listen to and learn from people unlike you in real life when you can. (And don't forget to pay the people you're learning from, especially if there's a virtual tip jar.)

4. *Pay it back*

The truth is, we're in a funny place when it comes to paying people back for their activism and emotional labour (see: teaching and educating you on their experience for free). Brands are more than happy to work with people like me because my work and identity happen to fit into the commercialisation of 'modern feminism', which is proving pretty lucrative for them (you can say that again). You'd be forgiven for thinking that brands want to be associated with women constantly at the moment, but not all womxn (I think the X has gotten a bit TERF-y recently, from what I've been told). They're often really not that inclusive. They are less likely to work with the LGBTQIA+ community and women of colour because many individuals from those communities are – quite rightly – very vocal about the discrimination and oppression they experience. They call out inequality and are critical of society, and for some reason brands are still distancing themselves from that bravery and honesty. (And sometimes these brands aid in that inequality and don't want to change anything about their way of business in order to be better. How is a brand supporting feminism when their entire board of directors is white and 60 per cent male?) I know so many incredible people who are educating others daily, but strangely, big brands don't offer them the same sort of jobs that they're offering a white woman who wears a 'This Is What A Feminist Looks Like' T-shirt made by modern slave labour, because so many brands still don't see anyone outside this very narrow archetype as valuable. To them, anyone outside that archetype won't make them money because they still see the consumer landscape as like them: a white upper-class or middle-class institution – and they can't grasp themes they haven't experienced. This is insidious racism, (classism) and homophobia – the idea that different experiences don't matter in the grand scheme of things. That's why it's our job to remunerate the people we learn from. With brands only platforming and paying certain types of people, we need to make a tangible effort to support those who don't benefit from privilege. Many of the womxn who we learn from on our social platforms are trying to educate us by putting out carefully crafted content and basically giving away a whole load of emotional labour and education for free. If we really care about women, shouldn't we give back, especially at a time where so many big brands aren't? If you can afford to, reach out to your favourite educators and ask if they have somewhere you can 'pay it back'. They may have a Patreon account (hi, it's me) that you can give to (also Patreon supports sex workers which is rad because if your feminism doesn't include sex workers what are you really doing?), or they may launch crowdfunding campaigns for projects they're working on. (Often they just take PayPal or Venmo and if you ask for that information, your educator will happily give it.) Keep an eye out and if you feel their work is valuable, show them the value of it.

If you fancy doing some essential legwork in this area, I suggest you put down my book right now and go and read Reni Eddo Lodge's *Why I'm No Longer Talking To White People About Race*. Go! Right now! Devour every page and spend some time filling in her Privilege Checklist. (You can also download Layla Saad's *Me And White Supremacy* handbook ... it's free, but you should definitely pay her for it.) **That way, you'll be able to see the things that have given you a leg up in life on a very obvious level, and the things that haven't been an obstacle for you, and don't stop there. Dive head first into educating yourself on your privilege and you'll be a better person and better activist for it.**

Aja Barber

(When Gina came to me with this project I thought, 'I think this is exactly what we need more of'. When doing work surrounding activism and inequality, we must all accept that we don't know everything. I certainly don't! But it's SO important not to pretend like you do because that sort of attitude really doesn't help anyone. There's nothing wrong with getting a little help. So, if you want to get it right, make sure your message includes the voices of people with less privilege than you, and you'll smash it out of the park. I believe in you!)

It was important for me to allow Aja to make edits, learn from them myself and show them publicly because white fragility, and the fragility that presents itself in privileged people, stands in the way of progress so often. We need to be less worried about making mistakes and more honest and open about making them and moving forward, and this chapter, hopefully, is an example of that.

5

THE ROLE OF SOCIAL MEDIA IN ACTIVISM

'Social media and technology can be powerful unifying tools if used well and used intelligently.'

Patti Smith, songwriter, poet, activist

THE POWER OF CONVERSATION ONLINE

Social media has gained a pretty bad rep over the last few years, and you can see why. For every supportive, tolerant tweet there seems to be an unending thread of acrimonious bigotry. Each scroll is flooded with sad news stories – it's enough to make anyone want to sit in a dark room in the foetal position. But dig past the bad stuff and you'll always find the good guys pushing conversations forward, organising events and lobbying for justice. Compassion may be quieter than hate, but it's reliable, always there and often stronger. Social media's ability to send information and conversations to as many people as possible in an instant has become one of the greatest tools for campaigners and activists in the last ten years, and although it sounds like an obvious benefit, it's completely revolutionised the way we receive, digest and share information, because it allows action to take place in new ways. Fifty years ago, a handful of issues were cherry-picked for the evening news and opportunities to interact with these topics were pretty limited. Now – if we want to – we can carry out acts of micro-activism every single day.

The last five years have seen online activism grow into a whole new beast. The #BlackLivesMatter campaign of 2013 started an international movement and ignited conversations about race relations, civil rights and white privilege. The #MeToo movement of 2017 spread like wildfire and is the biggest global conversation on sexual assault to have ever taken place, sparking a tidal wave of human stories that empowered women to speak about their experiences and encouraged men to reconsider their behaviour. These campaigns showed us the power of community; how a single conversation can activate thousands and trigger a shift in attitudes offline. I saw first-hand how the impetus to meet with, and listen to, women speaking on sexual harassment and violence changed inside the Houses of Parliament at the end of 2017, and my campaign definitely benefited from that shift. Social change has always been pushed forward by conversation and increasing awareness – they're called social movements because, like any other living thing, they need energy and momentum to survive. Whether your campaign is one of the biggest online social movements in history, or simply a small group of community members on a private Facebook group, interactions need a place to grow, develop and multiply, and social media is the perfect catalyst and measuring stick. If used correctly, it becomes a crowd of ambassadors shouting about your issue for you while you get on with booking meetings, writing press releases and strategising. It's word of mouth but on a far greater scale, and it's tangible. Conversations turn into data, which turn into ammunition for your cause.

CONTROLLING YOUR CAMPAIGN ONLINE

The media can be a gift when it comes to activism, but equally, it can be a curse. If you have made some ground with your message you'll find that journalists will write stories about your campaign or work online and often, you'll have no say in the matter. But wait, that's good, right? Free press! Well, as with everything in activism, there are always multiple sides to consider: what if the angle isn't what you want to push at that moment? What if it miscommunicates the objective of your campaign? It's a tricky one, because if you're anything like me, you'll assume the only way to be about your work is honest. But withholding small amounts of information to wait for the right moment, timing your communications and ensuring your message is consumed the right way is actually critical to playing the game, and the hard truth is that every single traditional media outlet has a political position, agenda and readership that they'll take into account when reporting. You can see this clear as day if you take one news story and look at it from multiple outlets; it's always presented with a different angle on each newspaper or site – everyone has their own spin, and will use charged language to push their agenda, completely transforming how you digest the information.

Here's one as an example: in 2016, then Prime Minister David Cameron outlined the UK's role in the refugee crisis after the government put out a press release. This is how two totally different papers reported it:

Daily Mail: 'Why We Must Not Take 3,000 Migrant Children'

Guardian: 'Britain's Role in Yemen Attacks Under Scrutiny'

Here, the *Daily Mail* focused on the importance of keeping out refugees, and the *Guardian* focused on the bigger picture, considering the UK's responsibility in the whole tragedy – incredibly different messages, and angles, yet both gleaned from the same press release. Now, my campaign made national news multiple times, yet thankfully I didn't have to deal with headlines that twisted my words. At the same time, I'd be lying if I didn't say a story's 'angle' often threatened to cause me and my campaign problems. At one point, an online newspaper ran a story about me being 'disgusted and disappointed' with the 'government's lack of action' when I was just about to get back in touch with the MPs I'd been working with. The danger was, I didn't want them to see that story and think I was prioritising talking to the press over them, so I put out a message on social media detailing how much I was looking forward to our meeting. I still have no idea where they got that quote from.

This is exactly where social media is key; it allows campaigners to have a lot more control over the narrative, which is critical because in activism optics are *everything*. Before social media, you'd be fighting with reporters and journalists to control the way your work was perceived, but now you have a lot more agency and can regulate how your campaign communicates your work. This is particularly helpful when things don't go as planned. Just take my run-in with Christopher Chope, the Tory backbencher who objected to my bill. When he objected to making upskirting a sexual offence in July 2018, I immediately confronted him in the Houses of Parliament. I asked him why he objected and then posted a statement on my Twitter explaining what had happened during our exchange, before we'd even left the building. I had the attention of the media immediately and they ran with it, which meant his defensive excuses for his behaviour fell on deaf ears. With social media you can take control, and that's a big advantage. Be aware that it enables you to control the narrative and shine a light on important matters, meaning you can broaden your reach and keep your issue on the agenda for longer than you would have been able to otherwise.

To help you out, here are my two top tips to make sure you're in control of your campaign online:

1. *Use Twitter as your official press channel*
If you use it right, Twitter will be an invaluable tool for your work. In the past decade, this platform has had incredible success because of its convenience and digestibility, but in the last five years especially its value to users has sky-rocketed due to it becoming an instant news resource for many. Non-partisan fact tank The Pew Research Center recently released their September 2018 Journalism and Media report, which listed Twitter as the third most popular news site – with almost 70 per cent of people consuming the news directly from their feeds for 'convenience'.* Even more crucially, journalists are onto this. That's why they are the largest active verified group on the platform. Poynter – a global leader in journalism – reports that they make up a quarter (24.6 per cent) of the service's blue-tick users and they're always looking for stories.† They want to know what's going on, so there's someone looking at all times, hence why #JournoRequest is one of the most consistently used hashtags on the platform.

This is huge news for your work. It basically means that if you need to get a message out, Twitter is the place because you can count on the fact that the media a) are always looking for stories and b) will make a bee-line for your account

---

* For more information, see www.journalism.org/2018/09/10/news-use-across-social-media-platforms-2018 (accessed March 2019).
† See the study at www.poynter.org/reporting-editing/2015/report-journalists-are-largest-most-active-group-on-twitter (accessed March 2019).

the second they get a sniff of a development in your story. Find and follow as many news reporters, writers, journalists, producers and editors as you can, make your account a clear landing point for your work, and whenever there's a development in your campaign, or you need to control the headlines, you can tweet an official statement, set the record straight or push the story forward yourself.

2. *Cross-pollinate between platforms*

When you're trying to spread a message you care about, it's important not to limit yourself by sticking to one platform, because different platforms do different things. You can spread your message more clearly and to more people if you use each platform correctly. Instagram is highly visual, Twitter is an information and news site and Facebook is pretty much what you could call your 'digital inner-circle'. Getting the most out of your online activism will mean posting relevant content across these different channels and sharing them across platforms.

Here's a quick breakdown of which content tends to work on each channel:

Facebook: This place is primarily built up of people who have known you throughout your life, so emotive and more personal content works well here. Your Facebook audience are far more likely to appreciate an honest look into what you're doing than your following on, say, Instagram and Twitter, because they are already invested in you. This is great news too because the 'share' feature is used more commonly on Facebook than on Instagram and you can generally push people that care about you to do more to help. Facebook is definitely the place for behind-the-scenes content or insights into your activism, but remember to always pair it with a direct call-to-action asking those who care about you and your work to do something to help you spread your message. For instance, Facebook was critical for me at the start of my campaign, as I asked my friends and family to share and sign my petition first before going public, in order to get the numbers up.

Do:

- Make any content to do with your activism 'public' so anyone can share it, and so that if people search for you that's the first thing they see (hi, journalists!).
- Keep it succinct. Short, bold video content performs really well on Facebook, driving higher shares and helping to tell your story in a more engaging format than just text. A recent survey conducted by the visual content platform Slidely showed that 47 per cent of consumers state that they now get most of their video content on Facebook, beating out YouTube.*

---

* For more information, see https://markets.businessinsider.com/news/stocks/facebook-tops-youtube-as-1-channel-for-video-content-according-to-a-new-survey-from-promo-by-slidely-1027446473 (accessed March 2019).

- Post your work onto Facebook communities. Campaigning about the environment? Why not post your petition on the wall of WWF, Greenpeace or other eco initiatives? Remember, though, to always think carefully about who you want to be publicly associated with and why.

Twitter: I know I keep banging on about this one but it's true! For activism, Twitter really comes into its own as a news site. However, due to its short character count, always remember that your message needs to be concise, easy-to-understand and as attention grabbing as you can make it.

Do:

- People love a photo. Social insights company Audience found that tweets with a high-quality image that helps to tell the story are 34 per cent more likely to get retweeted than a plain text tweet.*
- Keep an eye on conversations that are trending or getting a lot of traction – joining in with them could get way more eyes on your issue. Use trending hashtags to attract a larger audience, but always make sure they are relevant and that it doesn't sound like you're trying to piggy-back off something else!

---

* Find the statistic at https://postcron.com/en/blog/8-surprising-twitter-statistics-get-more-engagement (accessed March 2019).

- When adding a link to your tweet, use bit.ly to shrink it and make it trackable (that way you can find out how many people clicked on it and where they came from!).
- Slide into people's DMs. If you want to message someone but can't because they don't follow you (booo), have no shame – tweet them, explain the campaign, link to a good press or info story on it and ask them to share your post. If you don't ask, you don't get, and this is for the greater good!

Instagram: Instagram is a highly visual platform and it's a lot harder to share content here – they only introduced the 'share post' functionality this year for stories, but it's still early days for getting your posts to spread or 'go viral' on this platform. It's true that Instagram is a slow-burner when it comes to reaping rewards, and it doesn't have the immediate payback that you may get from Twitter in terms of journalists and media, but if you can build a following, you're winning. Followers of purpose-led Instagram accounts tend to be devoted individuals who'll migrate to other platforms to support you. Plus, this place does have the edge when it comes sharing real-time experience; its Stories feature gives you the ability to update followers with exactly what you're doing and show the human side of your work. On no other platform could I have shown people what it's like to head into the Ministry of Justice in real time.

Do:

- Use Instagram to start conversations and link up with certain communities, charities and peers in the space you're working within.
- Slide into those DMs like you do on Twitter! Instagram is a pretty friendly platform in comparison, so you'll find people are more open to chatting, especially if you have similar work in common. Remember, though, that this place is about relationships. If someone asks me a huge favour in my DM box but isn't even following me or engaging with my work I'm way less likely to do it.
- Use Instagram Stories to publish your real-life/ behind-the-scenes experience. People really respond to seeing the person behind the work, especially if the rest of your content is activism-led and heavy on stats, calls-to-action and numbers, which some of it might need to be.
- Use hashtags on your posts to add value to other relevant conversations and attract like-minded people to your work. Hashtags are super useful on this platform, so don't go without them!

The tactic of using multiple platforms for different purposes to discuss one single issue, and sharing or re-purposing content across the different platforms, is called cross-pollinating your content, and it can really build the reach and the awareness of your campaign. The more you can use clever content in the right places at the right time, and direct people clearly between your accounts as to what they need to do, the better. A petition may do well if it's on Twitter, but if it's opened up to three different audiences instead of just one, it's more likely to go further.

DEALING WITH ONLINE ABUSE

Online abuse can be any type of abuse that happens on the internet: whether on social media, online games or through your phone. Unfortunately, if you put your head above the parapet, stand up for something you care about and shout about it, you're likely to get pushback, even if you're fighting for a no-brainer. It's just the nature of the job – especially if you're a woman or part of a marginalised community. Recent statistics report that a woman is abused online every thirty seconds on Twitter.* It's super common, but like anything that's normalised, how common it is doesn't make it at all okay. It's entirely unfair that as soon as you start to discuss complex issues online, you are likely to receive at best mean criticism, and at worst violent abuse. The first step towards protecting yourself online is knowing what you're calling out.

---

* 'A Woman On Twitter is Abused Every 30 Seconds', Slashdot website post quoting a study by Amnesty International and Element AI, https://tech. slashdot.org/story/18/12/25/2232204/a-woman-on-twitter-is-abused-every-30-seconds (accessed March 2019).

1. Cyberstalking
This is the use of a phone or computer to stalk or harass an organisation, a group or an individual.

2. Trolling
Upsetting people, directing inflammatory comments towards people and starting arguments on the internet. The main objective of trolls is to upset or provoke a response from the readers of their messages.

3. Doxing
The unauthorised act of gaining and publishing a person's personal information. This could be family names, a home address, a phone number or financial details. Doxing is about having power over an individual by using their data. It causes stress, panic and fear over what others will do with the information. Mostly, this info is retrieved by hacking.

4. Online hate speech
Online hate speech includes written material, intimidating or upsetting behaviour, and images that depict hatred and target race, ethnic or national origin, disability, religion, sexual orientation, gender or other traits that are 'othered' by the status quo. Unfortunately, online hate speech doesn't have a legal definition.

If you're dealing with some kind of online abuse, the piece of advice you'll hear the most is 'just ignore it'. I find this so bloody unhelpful. It's not easy to ignore people directing vitriol your way, and ignoring a problem definitely doesn't stop it. The most important things you can do when getting online abuse are:

Collect evidence

Take screenshots of absolutely everything: info, dates and times too, and the profiles they come from. That is your evidence.

Talk to people about it

Don't suffer in silence. There's a propensity to tell yourself online abuse is 'not as bad' as real-life abuse because you're not face to face with the person. That's bullshit because everything is relative. You need a support system to deal with this insidious form of abuse, as you would any other type. Be honest with how you are feeling and talk about it often if you want to. Ask people to help you – you can even ask a friend to field comments for you.

Use the tools available

Sure, there are definitely not enough tools online to help you. Social media really needs to step up, but at the very least you should be using the tools you have available to you to help you deal. The block button is there for a reason: to help you create boundaries. So is Twitter's 'keyword' tool. You can enter words in your settings that do or might get sent to you, and Twitter will hide that sensitive content from you.

Don't try and educate trolls

Trolls have no interest in being proven wrong – they are literally there to get a reaction from you. I tried to educate people when I started getting online abuse, and it didn't work. Then I started doing it when I was drunk. Double didn't work. A great tip – which actually sort of works – is to write the response you would send and screenshot it, then delete. You will feel like you have got it out, but you won't have fuelled the fire.

If you need extra support, here are some amazing services doing great things:

https://paladinservice.co.uk
For any stalking issues, online or offline.

cybersmile.org
For any online bullying issues.

https://fixtheglitch.org
Not-for-profit organisation that exists to end online abuse.

CLICKTIVISM: DOES ONE CLICK COUNT?

You don't necessarily need to start a ginormous campaign to be active in moving society forwards. For some reason, when it comes to small acts of activism online, such as signing a petition, liking a post or voicing your support, that same old question returns: does it really make a difference? The thinking is that when we like a post telling us that by 2050 there'll be more plastic in the sea than fish, a psychological phenomenon occurs where we tick off the 'good deed' box in our heads without having made much change at all, and in doing so we give ourselves permission to go on to the next thing. This may be true, but throwing out clicktivism altogether? I'm not convinced. Sure, I can see how it may have made the image of activism far less romantic – your average Joe tapping his iPhone while watching *I'm a Celeb* is a lot less engaging than sashed social warriors marching for their cause – and I can understand the fear that we'll all get complacent and refuse to do anything other than sign petitions and like Facebook posts. But when I look at the amount a good click can do, I'm yet to be convinced that it's a desensitising monster.

Take the 2010 Haitian earthquake, for example: many people were moved by the human stories and donated online through a social media campaign, but few were concerned enough to get on a plane and travel there to help with the relief efforts. Nevertheless, all who were involved gained a whole new appreciation of the scale of the disaster.

Often in the argument against clicktivism, you'll see it pitted against offline work in a bid to make it sound frivolous, but that's a pretty unfair comparison. Activism is as unique as the person undertaking it. Different acts of social justice are started in drastically different ways, for different reasons; they have completely unique trajectories, and wildly different effects, which ricochet through a quickly evolving culture that can't be predicted. So, how can we compare one act to another? A march or rally, for example, can be valuable, but if held at the wrong time or in the wrong way, it can also be detrimental to a campaign. Thousands of names on a petition all signed with a single click can determine change, but only if the petition is then used effectively. There are too many varying factors to make a clear-cut decision on what's 'useful' and what's 'useless' in activism, and only those closely involved in the running of a campaign can know what is useful and why.

When pooh-poohing 'armchair activism', it's also important to recognise that not everyone has to be an activist, and looking down on Harry from Rotherham for not doing more doesn't help anyone. The truth is, having the time, inclination and drive to campaign, lobby or push for change is a privilege. I was lucky enough to be on a liveable salary, to live in one of the most progressive cities in the world, and to have an understanding of how the media works when I started my campaign, which gave me more opportunities for sure. Not everyone has that access. It's easy to write clicktivism off as a half-arsed attempt at social justice, but it's democratising activism and giving everyone, no matter who or where they are, the opportunity to make a difference in a small way. Plus, you might find that an 'armchair activist' will be exactly who you need when you want people to like your post, sign your petition and back your cause, all with a single click.

ONLINE VS OFFLINE

One of the trickiest things about campaigning is strategising. Knowing where and when to deliver your message is the difference between a successful campaign and one that never gets off the ground. We know social media is one of the best tools for focusing and seeding out your message, but does that mean your campaign should be primarily online? Does that mean offline activism should take a back seat for a while? At some point you need to get off Facebook and apply yourself, bringing your campaign offline. Know this: if you want to be successful in bringing about change, you're going to need to put equal effort into both social media and IRL. I'm often asked how I took my online campaign offline, but the reality was, I'd been running it online and offline in tandem from the very beginning. I just didn't make my face-to-face work public because it was important to me to gain the trust of the people I was working with (in my case, the government), and let them know that I was on their side and I respected our working relationship. To put it plainly, my online campaign was there to support my offline efforts and ensure I was taken seriously, and when I publicly revealed that I was working with the government, my offline work helped to fuel conversation online – a mutually beneficial strategy.

The lines do blur when it comes to offline and online efforts, but zigzagging between the two means a comprehensive campaign with both sides taking you seriously. People in positions of power aren't going to scoff at the person sitting on the other side of the table if they've got 250,000 supporters, and the online world is going to want to write about the young girl or guy who's bagging meetings with people in positions of power. Win-win!

The hard-and-fast rule is this: in the grand scheme of things your campaign should never be only online or offline. It should always be both in some way. Of course, at first, most campaigns will begin online and that's fine, but as soon as you're gaining ground and getting public interest, you need to make a decision on your next step. If it's bigger, more traditional media, then the key is to package up the data and use it to book TV appearances and inform newspaper stories. If it's to get into spaces with important people, then the key is to package up the data and use it to show them how many people care about this issue in order to meet with them. That should be enough to get your foot in the door. But if it's not? Head back to step one and build some more media and public pressure. Below I've outlined some questions that should help you pull some of your most valuable stats:

For booking media:

1. How many people have signed your petition?
2. How many times has your hashtag been used?
3. Which key people have talked about your campaign online?

For packaging your data into an email:

1. How many people have signed your petition?
2. Which media sites has your campaign/work been featured on?
3. Which key people have talked about your campaign online?

As well as these there will almost certainly be data that's totally unique to your campaign. For example, I counted up the number of stories of upskirting I'd been sent – whether from my petition comments, DMs, emails or comments on my social media accounts. I collected those stats and added them in too because it helped me to illustrate the problem, and they were the kind of numbers that weren't available online. Have a think about what makes your work unique and what information could help, but remember to ignore stats that the very people you're meeting with could find themselves with a simple search. You want to show your value, not regurgitate public information. The key to using social media is to gain insights into the issue that only you can bring to the table. Hopefully this section has got you excited about making change online!

Section Two

CAMPAIGNING

This section is here to *use*. It's not necessarily written for you to read A-Z, but more to look through the contents, and dip into what section you need to learn about. Write in it, highlight it – don't be precious about it!

6

GETTING STARTED

⁶ You only need one thing to start a campaign and it isn't cash, experience, a thick skin or the ability to use WordPress. It's passion.⁹

Lucy-Anne Holmes,
founder of 'No More Page 3'*

campaign
/kamˈpeɪn/
verb
Work in an organised and active way towards a particular goal, typically a political or social one.

W hen you think of the word 'campaign', you probably think of some sort of big, well-oiled national media

---

* Lucy-Anne Holmes, *How to Start a Revolution*, London: Corgi, 2015, p. 1

monster – but that's just one example. Actually, a campaign is just a way of describing an ongoing organised effort of any size. Whatever you're fighting for will determine what type of campaign you run. But whatever you're doing and whatever size, whether it's planting more wildflowers for bees in your area, working to get more women of colour into publishing, attempting to improve sex education classes at your – or your kid's – school, or trying to make communities more accessible for those with disabilities, if you're putting in consistent effort, have an end goal and are responsible for ensuring your work develops and progresses, then it's a campaign, my friend.

There are three main parts to any campaign, and without these three parts you'll struggle to finish what you started:

THE THREE As

1. *Awareness*
Educating people on the issue and getting it on the agenda.

2. *Advocacy*
Gaining people's support, and building an army to back your cause.

3. *Action*
Taking the awareness and advocacy you've built and beginning the process of pushing to solve the problem.

The amount of time these three parts take is wildly different depending on each campaign. Some can take months, some years and some a lifetime. How quickly they follow on from one another is also totally unique, and you may need to repeat steps. For me, awareness and advocacy happened almost in the same breath in terms of the public, and then I was on to action: taking it to the government. But once in there I had to go back to square one: educating and getting it on the agenda, and then gaining people's support inside the government. You may repeat steps, some steps may take longer than you expected, but they will almost always come in this order.

PICKING YOUR CAUSE

Choosing something to focus on can be overwhelming, so first write down your absolute core values. These are the very basis of what you care about, your fundamental beliefs – what's vital to you, others and the world around you.
Here are mine:

1. Honesty
2. Optimism
3. Respect
4. Integrity
5. Communication

Now, think about and write yours:

1.

2.

3.

4.

5.

Okay, now remember these because as we get deeper into this, you're going to find that there's a lot of stuff you want to change. When you're researching and wading through endless examples of injustice it can feel overwhelming, but what you choose should always be directly related to the above core values; the problem you want to solve will sit in direct opposition to them, and the solution you come up with should fit in with them. That's how you'll know it's something you care deeply about. Well, that and the fire in your belly.

When it comes to pinpointing what issue you want to act on, you need to be realistic. Big, broad problems are hard to turn into a campaign, and even if you think you can, they're less likely to be the kind of marketable, single-minded campaign that will get people on board and conclude with tangible change. The trick is to find a piece of the big puzzle to solve yourself, instead of trying to solve the whole puzzle at once. For ease and practicality, let's imagine that the method of picking your cause goes into two camps: 'active' or 'reactive'.

Finding your cause: Active

This is when you proactively go out of your way to find something to change. It's a method of sifting through the big themes you care about and finding a single cause to fight for within those themes. I think a great way to do this is a combination of 'distilling' (filtering broad problems into more manageable issues) and 'digging' (doing research on your chosen issue). So, first things first, grab a big fat notepad and your laptop, put on some excellent music, pour yourself a glass of vino and begin a mind map.

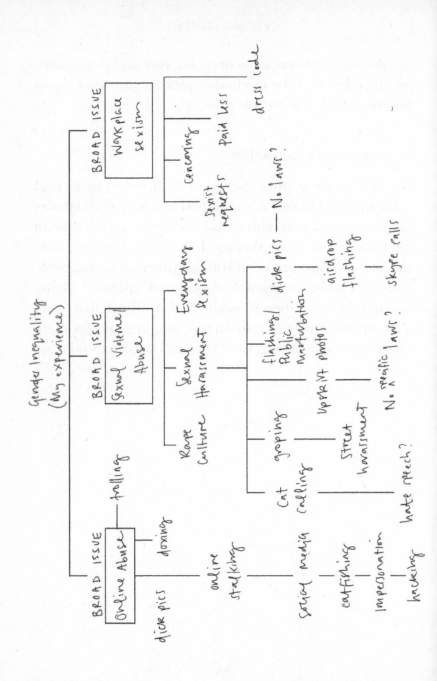

Gender Inequality
(My experience)

BROAD ISSUE
Online Abuse

dick pics
doxing
trolling
online stalking
social media
catfishing
Impersonation
hacking
hate speech?

BROAD ISSUE
Sexual Violence/
Abuse

Rape
Culture
Sexual
Harassment
Everyday
Sexism

Cat
Calling
gaping

Street
harassment

Upskirt photos

No specific laws?

flashing/
Public
masturbation

dick pics — No laws?

aircrop
flashing

Skype calls

BROAD ISSUE
Workplace
sexism

Censoring
Paid less
Dress code
Shirt
requests

At the top
Note down the two main 'Broad Issues' you care about. You'll recognise these as you rattle through different ideas because they'll be the ones that ignite a sort of fire in your belly. They should be the kind of subjects that you just cannot stop talking about after two espresso martinis. For example, let's take 'Gender Inequality' and 'Climate Change' as examples. This would be your first layer.

Second Layer
Try to explode your 'Broad Issues' out into different parts, or 'Sub-Problems'; e.g. 'Period Poverty', 'Sexual Violence/ Abuse' and 'Lack of Representation' could come under 'Gender Inequality', and 'Conservation' and 'Deforestation' could come under 'Climate Change'. This would be your second layer.

Third Layer
Continue to distil your issue down into smaller, more digestible parts of those 'Sub-Problems'. For example, 'Sexual Violence/Abuse' might now become 'Sexual Harassment', 'Rape', 'Sex Trafficking'. And under 'Conservation', you may have 'Single-Use Plastics' and 'Use of Pesticides'. If you feel stuck at any point, open your laptop and get reading about the last layer you wrote down, trying to find as much information on that layer as possible. Say you're researching single-use plastics – you might find out the amount of plastic coffee stirrers used every year. Now you're even more specific. Now it's even more doable.

Final Layer

Finally, you want to take one of the specific issues you have discovered and interrogate it. Choose the one that feels most interesting and relevant (to you and to society). It's going to become clear to you which issue you should focus on, as the mind maps that die pretty quickly are clearly not the ones for you (either because of inexperience or lack of passion; both fair enough reasons not to pursue them), and the one that you can naturally fill out more, probably is. Then, ask the below questions about your issue and research the hell out of the answers. I've added my answers below as if I were planning the upskirting campaign to help you out.

1. What are the causes of this issue? (list all)

Your answers:

My answers: *The male gaze, the media's objectification of women's bodies for male consumption, porn culture, rape culture, male fragility.*

2. What are the immediate consequences of this issue? (list all)

Your answers:

My answers: *Humiliation, victim blaming, perpetuating rape culture, online harassment, perpetuating the objectification of women's bodies for male consumption, violence against women and girls.*

3. What problems does this issue lead to in the long run? (list all)

Your answers:

My answers: *Violence and abuse against women, objectification of women's bodies, rape culture.*

You may see a lot of crossover in your answers, and that's okay. It makes sense! You're getting granular and talking about different parts of the same issue. But now? Well, now we're getting somewhere. You've picked your Sub-Problem, delved deep into it and are starting to understand it on a much deeper level. This is basic research for campaigning. By separating out information into causes, immediate effects and long-term effects as above, you get a better understanding of the issue. To start off, though, let's focus on the causes, because by getting to grips with the causes of the problem you can start to work out what the solution could be. If you can come up with a campaign idea that cracks one – or a few – of those, you're laughing (and changing the world)!

Tip: As you draw out your mind map, 'distilling' and 'digging', fill in as many layers and sub-issues as possible, splintering out as many times as you need, until you hit on something you find interesting. Generally, the more concentrated the idea, the better, because if it's concentrated, you can be more single-minded as an activist, and when you're more single-minded it's easier to set out a roadmap to get to the solution.

Finding your cause: Reactive

This is the form that my work took. In a way, all activism is reactive because you're always responding to the social, political or economic environment around you, but this is different to the 'active' approach above because it's less about one major act and more about setting the ground-work to become more aware, generally, so that when the chance arises to change something, you recognise it.

You are far less likely in life to notice injustices around you, or see things as changeable, if you haven't observed or evaluated your surroundings and how you feel about them. That's proven by just how little we notice the nor-malised injustices around us daily. Self-education and being aware of your privilege is an important pairing that, when engaged with properly, can help you to see the world and your environment through a different lens. There's a reason why the colloquialism that everyone loves to hate – 'woke' – was created. It's because when you understand your immediate surroundings and your society better, you become more awake to its intricacies: the ins and outs, the way it operates, the effects of it and how it became this way. I believe a similar principle applies in terms of noticing problems. If you're more aware of your beliefs, values and the society you're part of, you'll find it easier to notice when something doesn't fit with those beliefs or when there is an opportunity to improve on or change something.

We often make opportunities sound as if they're magical; an instant set of circumstances that make something pos-sible, presented to you on a plate and ready for the taking. Ironically, being reactive and recognising opportunities takes some work. It's all about being more conscious and aware of our own life experiences and what impact they have, but that isn't actually that easy. We're so used to going about our day-to-day lives that we very rarely recognise the things happening around us as problematic, or breaking our moral code, because they have *become our everyday*; even when the problem is staring us in the face, we can assume it's just 'part of life'. To be able to break that you have to gain the ability to recognise and question it.

Before I started my campaign, I'd been discussing,

thinking about and reading about women's issues, including sexual harassment, for a couple of years. I'd already woken up to the scale of the issue, what people were saying about it and how they were trying to stop it, so when I was upskirted *I'd already strengthened my ability to recognise the issue and, therefore, the opportunity.* The work and the act of being upskirted came together and turned into a catalyst to start the campaign. To quote an oft-cited comment from the American advice columnist Ann Landers: 'Opportunities are usually disguised as hard work, so most people don't recognise them.' You're one lucky person if you can stumble across an opportunity and instantly know how to grab it and turn it into something. Sure, some people have that innate ability, but I believe with most of us that ability often comes from a set of circumstances, and you can put those circumstances into place by *doing the work.* The trick is to get yourself into the mindset of being able to see problems and therefore recognise a solution as an opportunity – even if they come along at odd moments or in a disguise. This may sound hard, but it's actually incredibly doable. For recognising business opportunities, experts will tell you to observe trends and the economy, and look at competitors. But we're talking about the human experience here – about society – so it's all about soaking up real-life information and listening to real-life experiences.

To strengthen your ability to recognise an opportunity for activism in your life, take issues you care about – ones you always come back to, or can't stop talking about – and try these five things:

1. **Read about the issues from *different sources*:** books, newspapers, opinion pieces, Twitter, poems. If you're always learning about something from the same place, you're far less likely to find out interesting information and new perspectives, and therefore make valuable connections.

2. **Join online communities that care about the same issues:** that way you're introduced daily to new information and perspectives that could spark something. You may be thinking 'But I follow heaps of accounts on climate change already!', but remember, go niche! Look back at your diagram and follow the 'Sub-Issues' of that broad issue online. Search the relevant hashtags or the social accounts of editorial platforms and look at who is engaged in their conversations.

3. **Listen to current affairs and 'zeitgeist-y' podcasts:** they'll keep your finger on the pulse of the main issues and you'll be more likely to recognise a relevant (and timely) opportunity because of it. This is also a great way to get the news without actually watching the news, which, if you're anything like me, makes you want to cry.

4. **Read personal accounts from activists past and present:** nothing inspires me more than internalising advice from people I admire – people who have done the very thing I want to do. Gobble up their words and you'll find yourself thinking more like them, and sooner than you realise.

5. **Pay closer attention to what's going on in your relationships, your family, your friendships and your community:** this is critical if you're going to hit on a cause you care about. And it's simply about talking. Having frank and honest discussions with family and friends about issues you care about. We've seen the societal shift that's happened since #MeToo – women, for the first time, are speaking up about and discussing their experiences, and it's emboldened them to be able to bring language to define problems they have with society. If we're not doing that with the people around us, we're doing ourselves a disservice, because how do we ever drill down and identify the real issues that affect us? I'm not talking about a simple 'You okay?' though, I'm talking about making a conscious effort.

Trigger warning: sexual assault
In the summer of 2017 there was a wave of sex attacks across festivals in Sweden. Bråvalla, Sweden's largest annual music festival, was put under the spotlight when more than forty girls, many of them minors, reported being sexually assaulted or harassed by 'young men' at the festival. This was undoubtedly an awful story, but what followed it was a particularly inspiring response: Guy Dinners. Created by equality foundation Make Equal, '#guytalk' or '#killmag' is a call-to-arms to for men to step up, talk to one another and both break down the toxicity that leads to violence against

women but also create proactive changes from their position of privilege. The general gist is that guys host dinner parties with other men to discuss the important stuff, and can download free materials provided by Make Equal as a starting point, then give each other tough questions to discuss over dinner. Questions include complex topics such as sex, porn, love, ego, avoidance, fragility, violence and friendship, and 'True or False' questions include: 'I tend to take up too much space in conversation with others' or 'I often have a hard time admitting when I've made a mistake'. These dinners are the perfect place for ideas to thrive, because in a safe space with people we trust we can unearth, understand and develop the issues we care about more quickly and in a supportive and meaningful way. Taking it in turns to host a dinner each month (or whenever you can fit it in) to talk about issues you care about and problems you want to solve is a great way to become more tuned into injustices around you in your society or community, and therefore recognise them as opportunities for change. One month you could focus on one topic, and the next could look at an entirely different one from one of your guests. It may seem pretty simple, but marinating yourself with others in the world of broad causes that you care about allows for different opinions to be discussed, which may make you see things differently, form new cognitive connections and recognise negatives as opportunities for change.

To me, improving your ability to recognise opportunities is absolutely critical in activism: only when you can identify and run with an opportunity do you begin to notice the subsequent changes that unfold from it, and how to take advantage of them and push something forward. Once you begin, it's a domino effect, and that mindset aids you every step of the way.

Remember: Whether you work actively, reactively, or with a combination of both, there's always the likelihood that you may feel overwhelmed and not be able to pinpoint your cause or campaign idea. In that case, continue with the above – immersing yourself in the world of things you care about – and choose a simple personal goal in the meantime to keep the passion going. Head back to Chapter 3: People Power and tackle something personally: no longer using plastic bags, no longer shopping from fast-fashion stores, buying more from independent artists, etc. That way, proactive good will be part of your life as you take in information about the topics you care about. Once you've achieved one or two of those goals, you'll have spent more time on a cause, and may feel more confident in your abilities or have more information in your arsenal to unearth that issue you care about.

INTERROGATING YOUR ISSUE

When you feel like you have a focused issue, research the absolute pants off it. Your research should put a picture together of the current issue, how it's thriving, the conversation around it, who benefits from it, and who cares about stopping it.

Here are some interrogating questions to start you off on your research:

1. What are current conversations saying about this issue and why?
2. What have other countries (or, depending on the issues, other schools, organisations, communities, etc.) done about this issue?
3. How does our culture affect this issue?
4. What names keep cropping up in conversations about this issue and why?
5. Have any authorities called for a solution to this issue recently? If so, who, and are they in a position to help you?
6. Is there any information to suggest that this issue is making money for people in power and, if so, how?
7. Are there any examples of places or people who have tried to solve this issue in some way?
8. Who is affected the worst by this issue?
9. What are the main initiatives when it comes to this issue?
10. What are people asking to be done about this issue?

For me, this research was where I found my campaign: I researched upskirting and found out about its fetishisation in porn; the problem with it culturally in Japan and other highly technological countries; and the problems with it happening in schools and in shops. But then I stumbled upon the fact that Scotland had only made it a specific offence in 2010. I thought that was far too recent, so I checked on legislation in England and eventually realised that there was a gap in the law. It took a lot for me to realise I was right, particularly support from human rights charities and a very brilliant friend of mine who did some research and presented me with an idiot-proof report that corroborated my initial thoughts. To get there though, I'd had to do some research myself. You may need to reach out and ask for people to help you with your research. Not everything can be found on Google, or is presented to you in a way that you can understand. If I hadn't had a friend who could tell me this, I probably would have gone to a law student sympathetic to the cause and asked them to aid me. Interrogating is like being a student again, but there's no deadline. This is up to you! Ask questions about every part of your problem, go back over the causes, consequences and long-term effects of your issue, and ask 'Why?' consistently. You'll be in a far better position to understand the problem and therefore be able to come up with an idea that solves part of it.

FROM CAUSE TO CAMPAIGN

Now, I wish I could lead you through this bit by the hand, but unfortunately I can't tell you precisely where and how to turn your cause into a campaign without knowing the issue you're trying to solve and the causes and effects. But if you've been through all the stages above, the jump from cause to campaign should be the shortest in the process, because once you've discovered, for example, '2.6 billion coffee cups go into landfill every year', you can get to 'make my school ban coffee cups' or 'develop a new scheme for recycling plastic polyethylene', or you can come up with a marketing campaign to increase coffee shops' profits and make consumers use reusable cups. Once you have your specific problem, it's not a huge leap to find a specific solution. When thinking about your campaign and what form it takes, here are the main things to remember:

Your campaign should:

- Be a response to a problem caused by the 'Broad Issue' you identified
- Try to *stop the cause of a specific problem*. Whatever your problem, find the cause and create something that will disrupt that cause and therefore lead to a tangible change in the problem itself.
- Be something that isn't currently being done bigger and better by someone else. Sure, others will be fighting for the same thing as you – and you can join forces – but consider changing tack or your angle a little if your idea has already been, or is being, done.

Remember: Once you have a concept that could disrupt the cause of the problem, it's called an idea. Give it a name and a strategy (we'll get to that later) and it's called a campaign.

TELLING YOUR OWN STORY

Some of the greatest activists have used their own life experience to inform their work. I've said it once and I'll say it again: the human story has the power to activate people like nothing else, and you can guarantee that any issue that has affected you will have affected other people, too. Of course with activism, you'll always be helping others by forcing positive change, but it can also be incredibly personally healing to fight for a solution to your own past trauma, or something that has affected you – I should know.

If the issue you want to change is something personal to you, remember these three key things:

1. Be human

When you're championing something and want to become an authority on an issue, it's incredibly easy to shut off your personal quirks, change the way you present yourself and try to appear more 'professional' or play a certain role. Sure, it's important that people buy into your cause and believe you're the person to change it, but changing yourself won't do that. The very fact that you've experienced what you're trying to change does that for you. Who better to push for progress than the one that understands it most? As an activist you are a human. A fallible one at that, and one that's trying. While you'll undoubtedly toe the line between being respected by those who you need on side, and being liked by those who you need to support you, you should remember that your issue and your work will often speak for itself. You can still be you, and do great things. I wore bright pink and swore on TV and people still took me seriously, because I proved to them I could do it by being on top of things, reliable and strategic when it mattered. At the end of the day, if people underestimate you for whatever reason, more fool them when you turn around and finish what they said you couldn't.

2. Look after yourself

Activism can be emotionally taxing work at the best of times, but if you're dealing with the effect of some sort of trauma while doing it, burnout could be on the horizon. Always remember that you cannot do your best work unless you're healthy and happy. There is no way you will be able to approach this with a clear and happy mind if you're struggling. Your responsibility is to be kind to your body and mind, get help and look after yourself. You are the number one priority in every situation. The work can wait until you are ready.

One of the most important ways to ensure that you stay happy, healthy and motivated throughout activism is to build your support system. It's going to be very hard to have complete confidence and conviction in your efforts if those you spend your time with, or want validation from, don't provide support, or worse, actively make you doubt your passions or abilities. You are in control of who you let into your life and we all deserve a strong and nurturing support system around us to deal with what life sends our way. If there are people in your life who make you feel bad about yourself, de-prioritise them, alter the relationship you have with them, or talk to them about it. You're going to need a strong set of people around you if you are to take on the complexities and struggles of activism, and you will need people who you don't feel guilty venting to, who understand when you mess up or forget a plan, who show up for you day-to-day, not only when there's nothing better to do – people with whom there is implicit trust and support. Anything else is going to drain you, so have a look at the main relationships in your life and consider honestly if they are working for you as much as you are working for them. If not, adjust accordingly. You'll be so much happier and more confident for it.

3. Find your community

Whether it's medical, political, mental or physical, whatever you've dealt with will be something other people can relate to. Reach out and find others who have been through the same or a similar thing to you, and take what you need from that community and support system. Activism is never a truly altruistic act – you're doing enough, and if you need a support system to help you push through the tougher times of campaigning, ensure that you have an army ready to pick you back up. A wealth of experience, opinions and proof to back up the need and validity of your work doesn't hurt either.

KNOW. YOUR. STRENGTHS. (AND WEAKNESSES.)

If you're anything like me, you might think you can do this entire thing on your own. And depending on the scale and complexity of your campaign, you may be able to. But the truth is, however great you are at writing, communicating, marketing, selling, strategising, using social media, diplomacy, public speaking, and all the rest of what makes a campaigner a campaigner, doing it all on your lonesome could be detrimental – and not just to yourself, but the campaign too. To be the best activist you can be, there is one thing you have to know how to do: *know your limitations.* You can't set yourself up for success if you haven't recognised where you bring the most value and where you need support and guidance. When I began my campaign I knew within about three weeks that unless I got a lawyer I was never going to change the law. I didn't know the first thing about our legal system or changing legislation and for me to pretend I did would have killed my chances of success almost immediately.

Have a think about your strong points and write them

down. If you want to get serious about analysing it, try some good old SWOT analysis and think about your strengths, weaknesses, opportunities and threats. You can find a template for this online. After you've been honest about what value you can best bring to the campaign, think about what your campaign is going to require in terms of skillsets. You might find that many aspects could be doable: things like admin tasks and social media can be learnt if you've never had to do them before, but there may well be elements of your campaign that are far beyond your comfort zone, or which you know are out of the bounds of your ability at this point. For those, you need to partner with someone. You need to get someone on board who has that skillset so that you can ensure the best chance of success. My lawyer and I were a great fit on the upskirting campaign because we had clear roles. I took the brunt of the awareness and advocacy work by handling media strategy, social media strategy and garnering public support, and Ryan took on the heavy-lifting when it came to action by taking on the politics and the legal side. Of course, there was some cross-over – I was involved in a lot of the political meetings – but we both knew our strengths and our weaknesses. I wasn't too proud to learn how to think politically and Ryan wasn't too proud to let me teach him a thing or two about social media. Know your limitations and know your strengths, and apply them to your work accordingly. In any other job you'd have to, and this is no different. Unless you have a clear picture of your strengths and weaknesses, you are not going to be able to build a system where each part is working to the best of its ability. And believe me, you're going to want to build as well-oiled a machine as you can, because campaigning can get tricky at times.

But who do you bring in? Even if you know you need to? Well, that depends entirely on the theme of your campaign and where it fits into society, but if it's a lawyer you need, I know a thing or two about that ...

PRO-BONO LAW SUPPORT

Until I started looking for a lawyer, I had absolutely no idea that you could get law support without spending money. 'Pro bono' is the phrase that applies to professional work undertaken voluntarily and without payment. But unlike regular volunteering, it's a type of service that uses very specific professional skills to provide support and services to those who just can't afford to pay for them. First off though, when do you need a lawyer? Well, a good rule of thumb is:

1. Where law is directly involved
2. Where matters, e.g. regulations, are complex
3. Where you're dealing with organisations or people who are used to opposition or disputes

Now, it's important that I state this upfront: pro-bono lawyers are not necessarily easy to find. Having seen first-hand the (quite frankly) unsustainably stressful and busy lifestyles that lawyers lead, it's no surprise that many lawyers don't have the kind of time to offer pro-bono services on top of everything else that they do. It's not the easiest thing in the world to find the perfect pro-bono fit. It might take you having a whole load of meetings over a period of weeks until you find the right person to represent you, but when you do you'll know. You need to have the same values, the same view on the issue at hand, and you want someone who's going to amplify your voice, not take over. Someone who's going to be an extension of you and your cause, not the owner of it. Like with all of these kinds of choices, the only way you'll be able to tell is through sitting down and having a frank conversation and then listening to your gut.

But how do you find pro-bono law support in the first place? Well, unfortunately there's no 'system' per se. For me, I'd already started an awareness campaign online, started a petition and worked with some traditional media. Enough people were talking about the campaign that it could be considered 'public interest', and I used the piqued media attention to put a call-out on Twitter and to encourage any law charities, lawyers or legal aid societies to share it around. I also sent a whole bunch of emails to law firms that publicly advertised their pro-bono offerings. In the end I received three or four responses from lawyers interested in meeting up. It was immediately obvious from Ryan's response that he was the one to take this on. He offered to do whatever he could to support me, even if it was just a coffee, and he believed I had a genuinely legally sound argument. He told me it would be hard, but it could be done. I could immediately tell this was going to be an equal partnership, and it was.

Publicity, a sound legal argument and public support will *definitely* help when trying to pin down pro-bono legal support. There's no official route in, apart from digging through law firm names, trying different people and making the right connections, but there are a few other things you should try, and depending on what you need they could just do the trick:

Pro-bono organisations

These not-for-profit organisations – like the Aberdeen Law Project, for example – can help. They provide free legal advice and services to those who can't afford them, and they're pretty much available everywhere. Go to them when you know exactly what you need and have some momentum behind you. Public interest will be a deciding factor as to whether they put resources into supporting you. As with everything, you need to sell yourself and your campaign.

Recently graduated law students

If you need to partner with someone – like I did – and form a close and collaborative team, you're going to need to find someone who has the skills and is as passionate as you are about your cause. Let's be honest, a law student is more likely to want to take on pro-bono cases and get real life experience. And don't be fooled by age. My lawyer was twenty-nine, and I called him The Hammer for a reason – he absolutely smashed it. Most universities will have law societies, and they are a great place to start in terms of finding someone. You could also contact law firms with esteemed scholarships or training programmes and ask them to recommend someone who works on similar issues or cares about the issue your campaign is looking at.

For you, it may not be legal support you need. You might need someone to do admin because you're drowning in emails, you might need to ask a friend who works in the press to help you work out which media outlets to pick, or you might just need moral support before you go into a big meeting. Whatever it is, sear this on the inside of your brain:

Don't be afraid to ask for help.

Campaigning is fucking hard. And an activist who can ask for help is a better activist. You can't do it all and really, you shouldn't. This is bigger than just you. Look at your immediate circle first. Could one of your friends, family, extended family, colleagues or previous colleagues be helpful? If not, use online press, social media or career networking tools to help you locate those working in a certain area and to reach out to anyone who already has an interest in similar issues to you. Bumble Bizz, The Dots and Ohana are all good options for making connections with people you wouldn't normally contact for work.

DON'T BE AFRAID TO ASK FOR HELP.

SETTING YOUR CAMPAIGN GOALS

So now you have an idea for a campaign, you've researched the absolute hell out of it and you sort of know who the people are to help you make change, where they work and how that place operates. Well, now it's time to learn probably the most important lesson you can possibly learn about campaigning, and to really get it into your head I'm going to go all *The Shining* on your ass:

Play the long game and work backwards.
Play the long game and work backwards.
Play the long game and work backwards.
Play the long game and work backwards.
Play the long game and work backwards.
Play the long game and work backwards.
Play the long game and work backwards.
Play the long game and work backwards.
Play the long game and work backwards.
Play the long game and work backwards.
Play the long game and work backwards.
Play the long game and work backwards.
Play the long game and work backwards.

Has it sunk in? Nice. Whatever you're pushing for – stopping the sale of battery hen eggs in your local shops, encouraging universities to accept and support more POC, 'banning Photoshop on magazine covers' or banishing the tampon tax – the cold, hard truth is that you're very unlikely to reach the end goal if you don't have a strategy. I mean, sure, during the course of your work the original strategy may develop and morph until it's unrecognisable from what it was at its conception. Your plan might warp and change due to outside forces, but at the very beginning, you have to know what, and who, you're aiming for. You must *play the long game and work backwards*. More often than not, we don't play the long game and we sure as hell don't work backwards, because playing the long game forces us to have a goal that sits way past the line we're comfortable with. We don't want to go past it, and this way, we have to set what feels like an unreachable goal first. Starting is hard enough, so no wonder this is daunting. But it's the best way to work.

The Gatekeeper

Imagine the ultimate end goal of your campaign. There is someone or some people along the way who could make it happen. These are your Gatekeepers, and almost all campaigns have them. They are the people who can confirm the change you're asking for. For me it was the UK government, specifically the MPs and the Ministry of Justice team. Work out who these people could be for you and *work backwards*. They may be a head teacher, those who work for the council, your managers, a CEO of a company, the head of a union or your landlord. If you need to take your campaign to the council to make change happen, find out how the process works there, who could make that change happen (the Gatekeeper), and then work out the people you need to speak to and things you need to do to get to that Gatekeeper. Remember, there may be multiple ways of you making the change happen, so therefore there may be multiple Gatekeepers. As with everything in campaigning, *don't put all your activist eggs in one basket*. Try to have a few options, with a few Gatekeepers, that could lead to the change you want.

Once you have the end of the campaign – the objective – consecrated in your head, you can work backwards, using information about how that end goal works, and slot in the right moves at the right times, safe in the knowledge that you'll meet that objective because every move came from that end goal. Starting at the beginning without the end objective in sight often results in two things:

1. You'll end up putting moves down reactively and seeing where they go without a strategy, which means you'll add a lot of time to your campaign because you'll be meandering in the vague direction rather than as the crow flies.
2. You're in danger of mistaking single steps for a campaign because you can't see the bigger picture. A petition is a brilliant vehicle for change, but on its own it's just a petition and will more than likely just sit on the website doing nothing if you haven't worked backwards and made it a valuable vehicle in a larger strategy.

To help you work on this, grab a pen and paper and draw a timeline. Separate the timeline into your three A's: 'Awareness', 'Advocacy' and 'Action'. At the beginning of the Action section, write the name of your Gatekeeper(s) and consider carefully where it would make the most sense to approach them, to begin working with them to change whatever it is you are trying to change. This will probably be one of the most critical points of your Action stage because when approaching your Gatekeepers, timing is everything.

Under your timeline you want to write out all the vehicles you think could help you get to the Action stage. Here are a bunch of examples. Take any you think are relevant and add them to your list.

- Writing about the issue for local newspapers
- Reaching out to local charities
- Online petition
- Landing campaign media
- Social media awareness campaign
- Getting support from big names
- Gaining authoritative backing

Now, on that timeline in the Awareness and Advocacy sections add any relevant steps you think you'll need to get to your Gatekeeper. Don't worry too much about adding months or days to your timeline – this is just a basic structure to show you how you can start to build a simple roadmap to your end goal, now that you know what your end goal is.

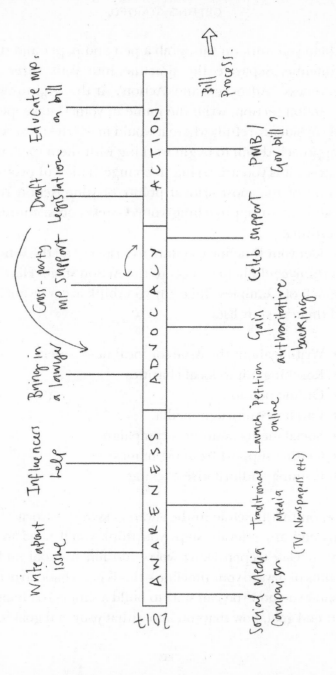

2017

AWARENESS | ADVOCACY | ACTION

Social Media Campaign
traditional Media (TV, Newspapers etc)
Launch petition online
Gain authoritative backing
Celeb support
PMB / Gov bill?

Write about issue
Influencers help
Bring in a lawyer
Cross-party MP support
Draft Legislation
Educate MPs on bill

Bill Process.

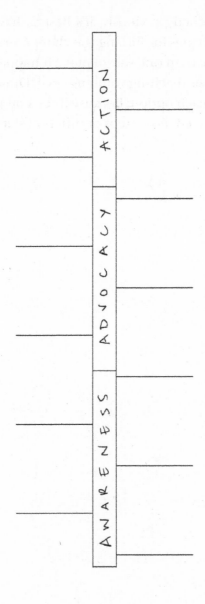

As I mentioned previously, it's best to have one or two different strategies for forcing the change you want – if you can find more than one way to make it happen, there's less chance of never reaching your end goal. Draw out separate timelines for each option, because if the end point is different they may need more steps or different steps to get there.

7

AWARENESS

awareness
/əˈwɛːnəs/
noun
Knowledge or perception of a situation or fact. 'We need to raise public awareness of the issue.'

You've got your campaign idea, you know what you want to say and you have a basic roadmap of how you're going to get to the people who can help you make that change. So, what's next? Telling people about it! I always said that for me, changing the law was just as important as starting a conversation about upskirting, because dialogue is what changes the collective consciousness of any society or community, and that is what engenders sustainable change, changes opinions and alters mindsets. Awareness of an issue can shift the social landscape just as much as the objective itself. You'll notice that a *big* chunk of this awareness section is about gaining public awareness and putting a bit of friendly pressure on those who can allow or disallow your efforts to become a success. The important thing to remember with this is that public awareness is more powerful than you think: when you put an issue on the agenda and use the public to help you do that, it holds people more accountable than if it were a private effort. Often – but only if done well – it forces people in powerful positions to prioritise an issue, and when this happens processes that may have been followed before can be adjusted. Take my bill for example. The public awareness and media hype around my campaign well and truly put it on the government's agenda, and due to the sheer amount of coverage and public pressure, our government bill was assigned a progressive timeline that meant it went through the process quicker than other bills might. This section is chock-a-block full of tips on how to get your brilliant idea out there and communicate it in the right way, at the right time.

COMMUNICATION IS KEY

When we try to change opinions, we hold micro-dialogues with others and discuss what needs to change. When we're campaigning, we're sustaining a macro-dialogue, sure, but it's effectively a large-scale strategy of micro-dialogues. You might be trying to ignite interest in a conversation about your topic in the public sector, you might be having private conversations and meetings with those who can help you, or you might be using media to start discussions online, but all of those smaller dialogues need to be thought out. Dialogue is, above all, what changes things. As our forever-hero Malala said, 'The best way to solve problems and to fight against war is through dialogue.'* But unlike regular dialogue, with activism your dialogue *has to be strategic*. It's about quality over quantity: speak to the right people at the right time and in the right way. So ask yourself these questions whenever you're putting a piece of communication out about your campaign:

1. Why am I saying this now?
2. Am I the person that should be saying this?
3. Who am I talking to here?
4. Is the angle of this going to help me get to my next objective?
5. Will me saying this help me or could it alienate me from those who I need help from?

Another important part of being a good communicator is the skill of knowing what you should and maybe shouldn't go ahead and do. There are most likely going to be times when you have to force yourself through uncomfortable communications to get the job done. For instance, if you don't like public speaking you might have to work on that

---

* For more information, see https://www.bbc.co.uk/news/world-24333273 (accessed March 2019).

to ensure your message is delivered properly. Personally, I don't mind public speaking, but I 100 per cent did not want to have to tell my story of being upskirted in great detail to strangers. However, this was something I had to swallow and get on with for the good of the campaign, because no one could tell my story better than me. It's also true that there may be instances when you are pushing yourself to speak on something, and actually, it doesn't need to be said, or it doesn't need to be said by *you* (this was a hard one for me to learn). The trick here is to think of your strengths and your weaknesses, and ask yourself this:

Will challenging myself here and communicating this be necessary to the campaign?

THE ELEVATOR PITCH

An elevator pitch is traditionally a sales technique designed to sell an idea to people effectively and get them on board quickly. But actually, it can be applied to activism in exactly the same way, as it makes sure you get your message across clearly and concisely in a confident, bold and passionate way. The idea is that you're in an elevator and only have the time you're in there – say, one minute – to convince your fellow passengers of your idea. These are brilliant for your campaign, but more importantly, they're great for you, because they teach you how to speak engagingly and get to the point.

They're also a godsend with your confidence, because not every room you walk into will be comfortable; you might be doing a high pressure presentation to people you need to impress, or maybe you're doing some short videos for awareness – a succinct pitch helps you set the tone quickly. Maybe you're sitting opposite a powerful figure who makes you feel a bit nervous. Fine – pull out the elevator pitch and it means that the first impression they get of you will be clear, comprehensive and convincing, not nervous and under confident. It means that your first impression is helpful to your cause by default, and that whatever happens, you at least have a succinct and convincing place to start.

Write down the answers to each of the following headers to form the main body of your elevator pitch:

1. The problem in a sentence
2. Evidence of the problem in a sentence
3. How you think this person can help
4. Why solving this problem is so important
5. A single unarguable statement

Here's a version of mine for reference:

1. The law doesn't recognise non-consensual upskirt images as a sexual offence.
2. The offence of 'outraging public decency' does not recognise this as a crime with a victim and many instances of upskirting cannot be prosecuted under this law.

3. We are asking for you, the government, to support this drafted legislation by doing A, B or C, and we'd love to hear other options of how you can help.
4. The reports on this are just the tip of the iceberg [introduce information on how rife this practice is].
5. As I'm sure you'll agree, the women of England and Wales deserve the same protection that the women of Scotland have.

Try writing out your answers, and play with them to form them into a passionate pitch. Go over them until that pitch is clear, concise and gets your message across within a minute or two. Remember that number five, the inarguable statement, is your chance to end on a really strong message. It sets the tone for the rest of the conversation. Take a closer look at mine and Ryan's statement: there's no doubt it's absolutely fair and true, but it's particularly effective because it compared our campaign to something that has already happened – something that an authority already saw as valuable. If you can write your unarguable point in a way that shows the success of your idea as a concept already, you're onto something. Plus, reframing your campaign as an opportunity, instead of a 'job to do', will always help.

Tip: Practise your elevator pitch on your friends and family and ask them to quiz you, argue with you and interrogate you. Ask them to play the role of someone who doesn't want your campaign to succeed or doesn't see the value of it. It might seem weird, but you're going to get asked tough questions along the way and you need to be prepared. Plus, your friend could come up with something you hadn't considered yet, and it may just make your work better.

FOCUSING YOUR ENERGY

Becoming a good communicator isn't just about what you say, but when you say it and what you *don't* say, too. The trick is to recognise when it's the right time and when it's absolutely not, depending on where you are in your strategy at that point, and that is all about focusing your energy. From my experience of campaigning and from knowing others who have done it successfully, I now think of it as a bit like chess: you move different pieces around, focusing on each one during each play, but being entirely aware of where the other pieces are, because everything is happening strategically to come together and push that one piece to the back of the board. You're unlikely to win chess if you only focus on the one piece you're moving. You need to focus your energy. You need to know which piece to move and when, and that feeds directly into communication, because you want to be clearly communicating which stage of the campaign you are at to your supporters and the people you want to work with.

Wherever you are on your timeline or roadmap, remember this: you may be focusing on this part now, but behind the scenes, you should always be setting up for the next stage.

You should always aim to be two steps ahead.

YOU SHOULD ALWAYS AIM TO BE TWO STEPS AHEAD.

The place that people think you are at in your campaign should be two stages behind where your head is at, always, because you're way less likely to hit your objective if you can't see ahead, and if the public and people in power are at the same stage as you, then who's leading this thing? Whenever you have one thing on the go you should always be silently preparing for the next two stages.

For example, if you're getting people to sign your petition, you should know exactly where that petition is going to go, why, and how you're going to get it there, and then you need to plan for the variables:

- Shall I use this to pitch the campaign to Gatekeepers, and if so, why?
- Shall I use this to get media, and if so, why?
- What happens if this petition doesn't go far enough to convince my Gatekeepers that people care about this issue?
- What happens if this petition does convince my Gatekeepers that people care about this issue? What's the next stage?

While this may feel like a difficult task, it's the difference between a successful campaign and a difficult, meandering one. Staying ahead of everyone else means you're on top of most outcomes, and that is critical to having an effective strategy.

As you're working on the campaign, and doing the heavy-lifting or planning behind the scenes, you need to make sure that you're clearly communicating what stage you are at *now* to whoever you want support from. Think of it as almost having a 'private' timeline and a 'public' timeline – the public need to see progress, and the best way to see that is to make them part of it somehow. You can do this a multitude of ways: with events, polls, petitions or, the easiest way to do it, online. When you ask for their help, you need to make it as easy for them as possible, and to do that you want to give them one job at a time. This is part of being a good communicator; making sure that your ask is clear and simple, while knowing what information to hold back (the possible outcomes, the next stages, what meetings you've had, who you're speaking to). The truth is, of course you want to be honest about where you are in your work, but people need to believe that there's a strong possibility of a positive outcome, otherwise they lose hope and therefore interest. So, with that in mind, if you hit a block or if your plan is delayed, you might want to consider keeping that information to yourself. Sure, vent about the fact that it's tough and ask for support from the public, but there's no need to always go into specifics. Often, going into the behind-the-scenes of your strategy is either too complex for people to digest online, or too boring. We'd love to think those who support us are interested in every single facet of what we're doing but that's just not true. No one needs to know everything about your work – so the more strategic you can be with the information you let out, the better. Remember the rules we went over of questions that you should ask during a dialogue? Get into the habit of asking them.

Main takeaways:

1. Stay two steps ahead (have a private timeline and a public one).
2. Question your communications.
3. Make your ask simple.
4. Give people only the information they need.

PUBLIC SPEAKING TIPS

Public speaking can seem incredibly daunting, but when something needs to be done that's going to help push your cause forward, you have to find a way to buckle down and do it – even if your chest feels like it's going to explode like that scene in *Alien*. Like anything in life, the more you put yourself through it, regardless of the fear, the better you get at it. At the beginning of my campaign I would sit there with my heart in my throat and I'd be able to hear it beating almost deafeningly in my ears. I was terrified. I'm one of the lucky ones though. I've always been quite good at hiding nerves, and I believe that the more you can do that, the more you realise you can get through scary situations. So, here are some tips for communicating clearly when you're doing the dreaded public speaking.

Prep your way

Public speaking can mean a million different things: speaking to the media, presenting to a board, delivering a speech, inputting on a panel, doing a reading or being interviewed. Each job is different, and each person is different too. Personally, I will always prepare ahead in terms of research, and with what I'm going to say. I like to have a few main pointers but generally I don't like to overdo it. Really fastidious preparation would mean that I'd have a rigid plan, and the worry of deviating from that too much would throw me off more than if I just went in prepped yet relaxed. On the other hand, I know people who need to carefully prepare everything to feel on top of stuff, and even then they don't think they've done enough. You will find out when you first start this work – and get your first few speaking jobs – what works for you and whatever that is, stick to it. Generally, if you're speaking from a place of passion and knowledge, and are the best person to speak on this issue – as I believe I was – you can prep less because you know what you're talking about and it comes from the heart. However, when I'm delivering a talk or workshop I will work hard on it so that others get the most value out of it.

When taking a public speaking opportunity, evaluate it with these questions and go from there:

1. Is this a conversation in which they just want to hear about my work and my feelings on the issue?

If so, do your thing and go in passionate and more unrehearsed, because rehearsing can mask your passion and we don't want that.

2. Could what I say here greatly affect the trajectory of my work?
If so, head in there with the main points you want to cover and a list of anything you won't talk about because it won't be helpful to your work. Be clear on these.

3. What's the one thing I want my audience to take away from this, or what action do I want them to take based on what I've said?
Think about that clear objective and then consider whether rehearsing or prepping is going to be detrimental or advantageous to this.

Slow down

I speak incredibly fast – like, joke fast – and when I'm nervous or excited I get faster and faster and stumble on my words. When you're nervous it's likely that you're going to say something you consider 'wrong': ACCEPT THAT. The chances are it's just a couple of words, it's not the end of the world – and Jesus, you have a whole load more to make up for it with. People like normalcy; they don't want to watch a perfect robot deliver a message with no emotion. Mistakes make us warm to people and realise they're human, so try and take the pressure off yourself a little. Alexandria Ocasio-Cortez recently championed the idea of 'Brave not perfect', and I second that. People want you to do well but no one is looking for flawless delivery – if anything, that's way less engaging. Accept that you'll make mistakes, and let it go. You're human. It happens. However, if you're really worried and do want a good hack: try to speak slower. It gives you time to think about what's coming next and enunciate properly, it gets your point across more clearly, and as communication is key, that's pretty important. If you're anything like me, actively trying to speak slower will feel like you're dragging out every word in a slow-mo-esque, dramatic-movie-scene style, so instead focus on your breathing. Taking breaths at the end of each sentence gives people time to follow you and means you don't have to concentrate on desperately trying to stretch out the words.

Be passionate!

Don't hold your passion back for anyone. You're the campaigner here for a reason – you care about this issue! Remember that and let your passion show – it's what will get other people on side. Of course, if you start to veer into anger or combative language, try to bring it back to positive and persuasive passion. Are you angry about this issue? Yes. But will communicating in a super aggressive way get people on side? Probably not. Use that anger, talk about that anger, praise that anger, but try not to become it when you're getting your point across.

Finish your message with a clear signal

In an interview scenario, I've found one of the trickiest things is how to know when the other person has finished their point, and ensuring they know when you've finished yours. Most long awkward silences come from the guest and interviewer not being able to read each other because a) you're a little overwhelmed by the environment and b) you don't know each other at all. I find that finishing your answer with a round-up of what you were saying is a great way to make it super clear you're done, and to keep the conversation flowing, e.g. 'So that's how it came about, really', or 'And I really, truly think that is incredibly impor-tant'. You see, you don't have to round your point off by summarising, just by aiming to give it a definite end, and this kind of language, however casual, does that for you. Plus, casual is usually better and makes people feel more comfortable. This can be applied to public speaking, pres-entations, meetings or any kind of formal situation where you need to command a room. Round the point off well to avoid trailing off and to ensure you sound way more convincing. When in conversation, ending with a question in relation to what you've just presented is a good tactic to keep conversation focused, or, when being interviewed, a particularly good device is to throw in a thoughtful nod at the end of your point – that always adds an obvious end point. You'll see me doing a thoughtful nod at the end of my answers A LOT on the news.

Look at one focal point

Don't let your eyes wander if you're speaking in front of a crowd or doing a TV show. It's way easier to keep your focus if you stay locked on the presenter or the interviewer, or the back of the room you're talking to, just above people's heads. Obviously, you don't want to ignore everyone there, but finding a neutral point to look at gives you focus and you're less likely to be thrown off by someone's baby crying or a couple of mates whispering to each other about getting another glass of wine.

Do whatever you need to feel good

Wear whatever makes you feel powerful. Have a drink before you go up there. Meditate before you leave the house. Ask your mates to come along so you can see them there. Do your make-up like you're going out for your birthday. Wear a suit. Wear comfy clothes. Do whatever you need in order to make sure you feel your best before public speaking and so you can be exactly yourself doing it. Play a more confident version of yourself, sure, but don't put on a suit if you've never worn one before. Wear what makes you feel good! Playing at being what you think they're expecting will only give you more to live up to and people can generally see straight through it. They want to see *you*, so give it to them!

8

GETTING YOUR
CAUSE OUT THERE

USING SOCIAL MEDIA

Ah, the old social meeds. A big one for activism, sure, but there's an assumption that you need thousands of followers to get your idea out there; an assumption that success on social media is the only way to navigate modern activism, and I'm here to say that just isn't true. I had absolutely no followers when I started, and for hundreds of years people have been disrupting the status quo without social media. There is no doubt that it's an unparalleled, amazing tool for communication and community, and not having your work online at all will be to your detriment, but any campaigner worth their salt knows that you *always* have to use more than one channel when campaigning – even the most successful modern-day social media activists go out into the real world and host talks, do panels, take part in discussions and set up meetings. As long as your campaign is both online and offline at some point, you're doing things right, because if campaigning is about anything, it's about using different forms of media and communication to complement one another. With your work, you might find that your online campaign runs parallel to the offline work all the way through, or maybe you'll start offline but end up bringing the work online in order to gain more awareness and advocacy. Perhaps you'll start online before transferring that interest to IRL, so that you can book media and speak on bigger platforms offline. Whichever way you do it, always remember the three 'A's: Awareness, Advocacy and Action. Look back at your campaign timeline, remember your end goal and work accordingly.

There may be a million ways to use social media to aid your work, but the most common use in modern activism seems to be a social media awareness campaign. Makes sense, as social media is all about community and connecting people. However, in a world where we are now digesting the equivalent of 174 newspapers a day of data – 200 times the amount we were twenty years ago* – one of the most crucial things about any online campaign is that

---

* Suzanne Wu, 'Ph.D. Student Calculates How Much Information is in the World', USC Annenberg website, 17 June 2015, https://annenberg.usc.edu/news/published/phd-student-calculates-how-much-information-world.

it's engaging and cuts through the noise. I hate to say it, but that's why branding is the bomb; there's a reason why Bloody Good Period are a stand-out charity against period poverty. Apart from the absolutely incredible work they do, their branding is bold, the name is absolutely killer and their visuals and tone of voice are completely consistent across everything. When you see them, you know instantly what you're getting – there's a sense of familiarity there. You see, it's not enough any more to just slap some information on your Twitter account and expect people to gobble it up, because online we're all fighting for space, and branding and consistency is what helps you cut through.

(VERY) BASIC BRANDING

A campaign's 'brand' is made up of many facets, including visuals, words, tone of voice, colour palette and values. Not every campaign needs a brand – particularly if it's a quick or reactive one – but if you're looking to build something long term, something that could even turn into a charity or initiative, it's a good place to start. Ultimately, your brand is how the world consumes your message and it should be totally true to what you're fighting for, so here are a couple of things to think about when you're branding your campaign:

Choose a bold, simple name that communicates your message

I chose the hashtag #StopSkirtingTheIssue for my campaign, which was clear and direct. Bloody Good Period uses genius wordplay that does what it says on the tin. Try and keep yours to the point and catchy.

Colours

Choose two colours that you think speak to the values of your campaign. Consider what you're fighting for and think of colours that could come from that, instead of taking inspiration from the negative thing you're fighting against. You want to keep the look and feel of your campaign positive because hope is a great motivator. Steer clear of heavy or jarring colour combinations, and instead go for something that reflects hope for the solution, not anger at the problem. Now, the critical thing to remember here is that if you have no idea how to navigate the design world, it's time to ask for help! Reaching out to design students or a friend for help could be really useful – but again remember this doesn't have to be fancy. Mine was literally the hashtag #StopSkirtingTheIssue in red over an image. That's it. As long as it's a high-quality image, fairly modern looking and eye-catching, you're good to go. Don't agonise over this, but don't rush it either.

Once you have a basic logo and colour palette, design a few simple visuals that you can pop across your social channels:

- A Twitter cover photo
- A Twitter image with basic info that you can pin on your profile
- Some Instagram stories you can use on your profile's Highlights (as, like Twitter, they stay pinned to your profile and are one of the first things people see)
- An image for a Facebook page or group (display image and cover photo) if you think Facebook could be viable for building a community around your campaign

Remember not to go too overboard with your branding on everything, especially if you already have existing social media pages, as people follow you for a reason, and generally when it comes to activism people respond best to *people*. The branding is just there to communicate your idea and give anyone who wants to write or talk about it somewhere to go to find out some basic information. It's particularly useful if journalists pick up on your work or if you're asking someone to tweet about your campaign – this way they can just go to your profile and retweet your pinned tweet with all the info there and ready to go!

Now, every single social media campaign will be different. In terms of the type of content you put out, the timing and how you orchestrate it, that's down to you. But this is a tool after all, so there are some basic principles that you can adapt to fit the purpose of your campaign, which will help to drive it forward and make the process easier for you.

I'll run through them here. Remember, though, that this campaign is yours. It's personal. And it should be designed around your objectives, as discussed earlier, so yours may run differently from how mine did, and that's great!

A hashtag

I considered creating a website for my campaign *so many times*, but eventually decided against it because of lack of time, resources and money (life, eh?). The truth is, unless your work is going to last for years and be part of multiple initiatives (see: March For Our Lives), a hashtag is probably enough. It brings every piece of content related to your work together, and, if you're clever about it, it can educate viewers on your issue at a glance. Now, if I'm honest, I could have chosen better timing for my hashtag – I launched it late because I was so overwhelmed at the start of my campaign and had no idea what I was doing. However, once I began to use it consistently, and as the official headline for an editorial series telling victims' stories for Refinery29, it began to get picked up and became fairly effective. The actual structure of the hashtag was well thought through, too. #StopSkirtingTheIssue was a call for the government to stop delaying a change in legislation. The subtle play on words gave an idea as to what the campaign was about, and it was unique enough that my content didn't get lost under 300,000 previous uses.

When starting to plan your work, you must think carefully about what your hashtag could be. Make it easy to use and understand, make it catchy, and please read it through and look at the composition of the phrase too. We don't want a repeat of #susanalbumparty or #LoveDP. Probably the most important rule with hashtags during campaigning is to learn from my mistake and LAUNCH WITH IT ON DAY ONE. Because I was slow on the uptake and only started using mine properly months into the campaign, I couldn't follow – and therefore be involved with and use – the conversations happening around my work from the beginning which meant I missed a lot of opportunities to join, and take advantage of, conversations and community happenings online. Because I didn't launch it on day one, the hashtag wasn't immediately synonymous with my work, so people didn't always use it and I couldn't locate anything coming off the back of my campaign. It also meant there was far less content and information on my campaign for people to access easily. If I'd used it from the get-go, anyone who saw it could, in a single click, have accessed a whole library of information on my work that they could read, like and share (free promo!). Therefore, it's pretty key that you use it consistently, urge others to use it and make it a big part of your branding. It should be central to all of your messaging. Don't type without it.

Once your campaign or movement is underway, do what I missed out on and make the effort to effectively follow your hashtag to see who's engaging with your work and cares about the issue. That way you can make connections and grow your reach. Doing this, though, is not just about searching your hashtag. Instead, make sure you download social analytics tools like Keyhole or Tweet Binder as soon as you start using your hashtag. These social media listening tools will track when, how, where and how often your hashtag is used, giving you data that can prove people care about your campaign. Once you see people using your hashtag, work hard to start conversations with them and in doing so you'll create more noise around it. Maybe someone posts your hashtag with a story that relates to your campaign – work with them to tell their story! Maybe someone of note shares something related to the campaign with the hashtag on – contact them, start a relationship and keep them in mind for when you need a big social media push. Try to respond to everyone who uses it at first, and direct them to a simple action that could help your campaign. As it grows, cherry-pick the most valuable conversations to become involved in. It might seem simple, but if used cleverly a hashtag can be #invaluable.

Planned messaging

A study by Microsoft Corp.* found that our attention spans stand at eight seconds long – one second shorter than your average goldfish and four seconds down from what it was in 2000. But what about when you're asking someone to do something online? Well, it's much likely to get shorter. Communication is everything in activism and the most

* For more information, see http://time.com/3858309/attention-spans-goldfish/ (accessed March 2019).

detrimental thing you can do is expect people to wait to find out about your cause, the problem behind it, and how to help. If they're not captivated in the first second or two, they're gone (possibly forever). In the early stages of launching a campaign or initiative, you're going to be trying to build support for your cause online, so the hope is that each time you put out a piece of content, someone new will hear about your work. Because of this, you have to always assume there's going to be someone seeing your posts without any context. Even if you've written the message one hundred times and feel like 'your followers' get it, consistency and clear repetition is the key. Next time you're tweeting, writing a petition bio or planning Facebook ads, combat confusion by asking yourself these five things:

1. Is the most emotionally engaging part of this message at the beginning?

2. Do they have enough information to care, but not enough to feel overloaded?

3. Is it 100 per cent clear what I'm asking people to do?

4. Is the tone of voice consistent with my other work?

5. Is there a clear and simple call to action?

If you can answer yes to all five questions, you're on track with your messaging.

If not, I've answered the questions below using my own campaign as an example to help you gain clarity. Read them through and then note down your own answers below mine.

1. *What is the most engaging thing about my campaign?*
I was upskirted and even though I handed the man in, the police couldn't help me.

2. *What do I want people to know about my campaign?*
Taking upskirt photos without someone's consent is a sexual offence in Scotland, but not in England and Wales.

3. *What, exactly, do I need people to do in this moment?*
Support my fight to change the law.

4. *What is the clear call to action here?*
Head here [link] and sign to ask MPs to make upskirting a sexual offence.

Next, take your answers and try to form a concise, clear sentence with them. Try playing around with a few different formats such as a tweet, the beginning of an email and a media quote, and watch how successful activists Munroe Bergdorf or Stacey Abrams speak online – you'll notice they have a consistent tone of voice, they stay on message and they engage with people quickly.

E-petitions

When you're asking for something to change you need to be able to show, in numbers, how many people support that change. A petition is usually somewhere in the beginning of the fight, but it's a critical part of the journey and should only be deployed when you have enough support to get some signatures. A petition is a visual representation of public awareness and public pressure – much like a march, but digital. And, as we've previously discussed, traditional processes can be adjusted if a subject has 'high public interest', so showing that clearly is imperative. However, choosing which petition website to go with is not as clear-cut as you may think. They don't necessarily all do the same thing. That's why it's far more valuable to choose your petition site for its functionality first and foremost. Ask yourself these four questions when you're picking your platform:

1. What kind of tools do they have that can help extend my reach?
2. Do they update signees on changes to the campaign?
3. Will they aid me in getting my campaign out there or just leave me to it?
4. Do they have a large (and real) following on social media that they can use to help me?

You can work all of this out by looking at their follower count and then the activity on their account. If they have a lot of followers (thousands) there should be a healthy amount of likes, comments and activity. If they have a lot of followers and not much activity at all? Something's not right. For my campaign, I chose Care2 – a US-based social justice site – because they seemed committed to their campaigners and had some very helpful functionalities; my original petition was to set the tone and call for a change in the law. It had regular functionality, with people signing and commenting. However, halfway through my campaign I wanted something more 'active', and asked the team about something that had formed part of my decision to choose their platform. They offered a petition that allowed me to send pre-written emails to MPs every time a person signed their name by using a database. We set this up and used it through the campaign and it worked incredibly well. Currently, this petition stands at 7,005, which means 7,005 emails were sent to British MPs – of which there are only 650. That's ten letters per MP (sorry, guys!). Now, this functionality was killer because it gave maximum impact with minimum effort from signees, which, when you're talking digital, is the Holy Grail. Would the government's very own petition website have allowed me to do that? Hell no! They wouldn't have wanted to send themselves annoying, letters would they? If I'd gone straight to the Parliament petition website there's no way I could have done that. So the lesson here is that it's always worth thinking strategically instead of jumping for the first option.

The key to finding the perfect platform for your work is to reach out to a bunch of sites and do your research. Many petition websites will also dedicate an actual human to oversee your petition, as it benefits them to be involved in a campaign of public interest, so don't be afraid to collaborate with them and ask them how to build on the interest. The lovely Beth from Care2 was my point of contact (hi Beth!), and we worked together to create Facebook ads to promote the petition to the right audiences when its numbers started to grow – they often have a budget and it never hurts to ask. When choosing a petition, you might find yourself reading the online reviews, but remember

80 per cent of them come from signees not campaigners, and the general public hate petitions because they clog your inbox and ask for money. Don't take these reviews as an indication of whether these sites are useful in terms of activism – leave that to me!

To help you choose, here are three platforms you might want to consider and why:

change.org
This site is a humongous platform with, as I write, 247,936,355 regular people taking action, and they're very good at shouting about their campaigners. This is a good sign because it means they'll help you with press around your work. They also have an interesting feature called 'Decision Maker'. When you start a petition with them, they'll ask you to designate 'Who can make this change?' This could be an elected official, government body, or leader of a company – this is your 'Decision Maker', their version of what I call your Gatekeeper. For me, that early in my campaign, I wouldn't have known exactly who the person with the power to make the change was, but I would have gone with a powerful figure with the ability to push a bill forward – the Minister of Justice, for example. When you input this, change.org will have a dropdown menu of people. If they're in that list, the site has an email for them already, but if they're not you can find it online and input it yourself. Now, the point of this feature is that your Decision Maker will be notified periodically as your signature count rises. This is useful, because although it may not

help you get the job done, it will definitely help you start a relationship with a powerful person, meaning you'll have made initial contact and won't have to go in and pitch your campaign cold.

petition.parliament.uk

The official government petition website is the first option for a lot of political campaigners, and I can see why; the common perception is that if you're trying to force change, why not engage directly with the most powerful people in the land? The site encourages petitions with the promise of a 'response from the government' at 10,000 signatures and says petitions 'will be considered to be debated' at 100,000. If you look at the small print, though, you'll realise that not all petitions are guaranteed a *useful* response and there is no automatic parliamentary debate based on a petition reaching 100,000 signatures. They'll consider them, sure, but the process isn't mapped out for you if you reach 100,000, hell, the next step isn't even guaranteed. I was implored by countless people at the beginning of my campaign to use this site because they were absolutely convinced my petition would be debated. That may have been true because of the media interest in my work, but I also knew, from working in close proximity to them, that government time is strictly allocated and MPs receive hundreds of thousands of petitions a year, so a petition alone is unlikely to get you government time and in the room with the right people. You see, they don't make big decisions based on just petitions: at the time of writing there are currently 31,731 petitions on the site, but only sixty have been debated (and, of course, it depends how you define 'debate'), and of the ten most successful campaigns of 2016, four were denied a debate and none have succeeded in their outcome or implemented real change. It's important to remember that if you're running a political campaign, at some stage you might want to hurry things along or put some friendly pressure on them, and that might be hard to do from their own petition site. If your petition is there, you're sort of playing into their hands by allowing them to control part of your campaign. Because of this, independence is often more valuable. Setting aside those reasons to go with an independent site, there is one valuable functionality on this site: the Petitions Committee. They review all petitions and do have the power to pressure the government from the inside – which could be useful, depending on what you're campaigning for.

38degrees.com

38 Degrees has been responsible for a few heavyweight campaigns you will have heard of; the organisation worked to save a public forest from being sold for deforestation in 2011 and it made the 'Save The NHS' campaign a site-wide priority, making funding cuts more difficult for the government. They have done some good work, and it's clear that their success comes from the individuals who run the site supporting their campaigners. This place is a true community petitions site, not a faceless platform: you

can see and interact with everyone who works on, volunteers or runs the site. This means one-to-one support with your petition, which is an absolute godsend. The names of everyone who runs 38 Degrees are listed on their site, so you can also give them a tweet or an email if you need anything along the way. 38 Degrees also hands power over to its campaigners, asking them to vote on which campaign should be the site's next priority. This means that if you can get your social following to vote for you, sell your petition well and convince the site's users of its value, it could go stratospheric!

GETTING YOUR CAMPAIGN TO THE RIGHT PEOPLE

Okay, so we we're talking awareness here, but this is great for awareness *and* advocacy. Getting eyes on your cause and campaign is the real beginning of pushing for change, and it's an important step because if you can get the *right* eyes (more important than the number of eyes!) on your cause, then you have laid some strong groundwork for the rest of the campaign. This works a little bit like social media: you could have 100,000 followers, but if 80,000 of them are people who don't necessarily have great empathy for your cause, it's not going to do much. When getting your work out there for the first time, you're looking to specifically target the kind of people who care about this. There will come a time for you to get broader public support, but in order to have the right tools to do that you're going to need an army of people who care about your cause.

To work this out, take your campaign and break it down into different – and relevant – themes and groups of people. For example, for my campaign against upskirting I could have broken it down into the following groups of people:

- Women's rights charities (because this was a safety issue for women)
- Music festivals (because this is a big problem in those spaces)
- Violence against women charities (because this could lead to violence against women)
- Women in politics (because my end game was political)
- Female celebrity culture (because upskirting from paparazzi is a problem for celebrities)
- Anti-porn culture initiatives (because upskirting was born from online porn)

Once you've broken it down, you can easily identify people, charities or initiatives to reach out to who would be sympathetic or interested – if you've already done research into the issue, then you'll probably have some ideas in your head about who to contact straight away! Make a list of every person of note, charity initiative, ambassador, journalist, politician, writer or artist you can think of that deals with these issues, and see this list of people as your first awareness strategy: follow them, pay attention to – and note down – anything they talk about that is relevant to your cause, and ask them if they'd be happy to use their platform to support your cause and get your message out. The chances are they'll be happy to help, because it intersects with their work directly and therefore it won't look unusual on their social feeds or as part of their overall communications strategy.

Bear in mind when reaching out to people that *everyone is busy. No one has time for you, so you have to sell it.* Now, I know this sounds harsh, but I've always found that if you start from that perspective you generally have more success (i.e. replies!) because you're more likely to take their limited time into account and present them with something digestible and engaging. Another thing to watch out for is that, in writing, there's a fine line between enthusiastic and rude. There's also a fine line between being professional and un-engaging. You never want to seem unprofessional or not legitimate, rather someone who is engaging, passionate, who knows their shit and can make things happen. So be friendly, but not too familiar, and be authoritative but not too clinical.

WRITING A PERSUASIVE PITCH

1. *Use their name! (But be respectful.)*
Don't open an email with 'To Whom It May Concern'. If you didn't do enough research to even find their

name, subconsciously they probably won't be convinced you can change whatever it is you're trying to change! Generally a simple

> Hi Lucy,
> Hope you're doing well!

works a treat if it's not a very official email, and

> Dear Mr/Ms [name]
> Hope this email finds you well.

is usually what I go for when I want something more official. Critically, official emails were sent through Ryan, my lawyer, for the duration of our campaign. The backing of his law firm Gibson Dunn gave the message more authority and therefore it was more likely to be prioritised, so here are some tips to ensure your email holds weight:

- Set up an official-looking signature for the bottom of your email. Your name and title in italics, your contact number, and your social handles, campaign website or hashtag with a logo will look official and give them some context
- Set your email to 'High Priority' (but only if it is actually high priority)
- If you've copy and pasted anything into the email window, you might have picked up different fonts and sizes that you can't see. Make sure you

de-format all text so that it doesn't come out the other end looking like a ransom note.

2. *Introduce yourself in a sentence*
For example:

> Just to introduce myself, I'm Gina Martin, and after becoming a victim of non-consensual upskirt images at a festival last year I've been campaigning to make upskirting a sexual offence in England and Wales.

You'll notice how I didn't just say 'illegal', I was specific in order to demonstrate I know the legalities of what I'm trying to do. Also, I didn't say 'I'm hoping to', or 'I'm starting to' – don't be apologetic; be confident and bold!

3. *Let them know you appreciate and understand their work*

> I have been aware of your essential work for a long time, I specifically loved your [fill in what you loved], and I wanted to ask if you would consider supporting my campaign. I think we could work really well together!

4. *Make it crystal clear what you're asking them to do and give them options*

> There are a number of different ways we

could work together, so please let me know
what you think is doable.

Notice how I specifically didn't write 'how you can help'
so as not to make it sound like I'm asking everything from
them and giving nothing back in return.

1. A post on your social media platforms
encouraging your followers to sign our petition
would be amazing.

Here you can write an example post for them with the right
hashtags, handles and the right word count, etc. Make sure
to detail to them when you need this to go out.

2. I know you do fantastic events and would
love to be part of one. If there is any
space for a discussion around the issue our
campaign highlights or the campaign itself
please let me know!

3. I would love to partner with you for a digital
campaign that unites us and draws attention
to the work of both of us.

Give them one content idea: could it be a series of videos?
Could you interview people who have been affected by the
issue you're talking about? Get creative.

Giving people options not only gives you more chance of a response but it ignites ideas in their heads of how they could work with you, too. Generally, I'd stick to three options to ensure sure your email isn't a crazy long and intimidating read. Plus, you want to make these options a sliding scale of effort for the person:

- Super easy to do from their phone
- Something fairly easy but that requires a little more work, e.g. a quick video clip you can use
- Something that takes more work and is a little longer term

5. *Give them some easily digestible information about your campaign* (but don't give them anything you don't want to be public. Mistakes happen!)

> Currently I'm trying to gain public support against upskirting, so that when I head into Parliament **(again notice I didn't say 'because I want to show the government' – confidence, people!)** I can show the Justice Minister what a problem this really is. Our aim is to either have an MP table a Private Members' Bill or table a Government Bill with the Ministry of Justice.

At the very start of my campaign, when I was trying to create awareness of the issue of upskirting, I must have sent *hundreds* of emails like this and, if I remember rightly, around five charities and three people with fairly good followings offered to help me. It's a numbers game, but one thing is for sure, the more you put in, the more you get out.

Remember: Some of the options you give them will help you garner public support and some of the options will help you garner industry/professional support. Generally, you'll need both of these, but it's worth checking in on yourself and considering what you need more of now and what can wait till later. It's never a bad thing to make connections with the people you reach out to though, even if you're not ready to use them. You can keep those relationships going behind the scenes until you need them and focus on the public support for now if you think that's best – remember, focus your energy!

REACHING YOUR COMMUNITY

I've banged on about the importance of the human story enough already, but it's everything, and if you haven't reached out to people who have experienced the effect of the issue you're fighting already, now is the time to do it. I mean, if you're someone who has experienced the problem then these people should be central to your work. Make it one of your main tasks to find those who have experienced, understand or have been affected by what you're campaigning against and help them to tell their story in some way. How you work with them depends on your campaign – you could host an event where they share their experiences, pitch their stories to a website as an editorial series (with their consent, of course), or create a social campaign with them. Get creative and collaborate, but remember you should *always* be looking to do these three things when working with people who have experienced what you're fighting against:

1. Understand the problem better
2. Ensure your supporters understand the problem better
3. Empower the individual

Working within and with a community of people who 'get' what you're trying to change means being responsible with their stories. But if you are, there is nothing like being part of a group who completely understand the problem to make you feel motivated, and to help you get to the end goal. For me personally, connecting with young girls, women and people who had been upskirted and sharing that understanding was a huge motivator. When it got really tough and I was struggling to manage everything, or handle the pressure, those conversations were what kept me going, because it was way bigger than me. I really believe that broadening out your understanding of an issue by talking to others and learning from them makes you better at your job. For me, taking myself out of the picture and using those people as my motivation made it way easier to show up and push harder.

HOW TO WRITE A PRESS RELEASE
(and get it out there)

A press release is a concise and simple one-pager that details newsworthy info to journalists, press offices, producers, writers and big media arms like the Press Association before anyone else; a first look at a story that no one in the media knows about yet. Generally, a press release will include information on the story, quotes from relevant people, and instructions on a specific date and time to release it, as well as all the relevant contact details for follow-up and further information. But its biggest value is that *it allows you to control the angle of the story before any media get hold of it*, and that is gold dust. But hey, just like gold dust it's rare, so you should only use a press release when totally necessary and you have big news, otherwise you just become the person who sends out average press releases, and we don't want that: your relationship with the media is incredibly important when campaigning. Our rule was generally that if the media wasn't a specific part of our strategy at that point, and unless we had *huge* news, we didn't send one.

EMBARGO DATE SO THEY KNOW EXACTLY WHEN IT IS OKAY TO RELEASE THE INFORMATION: E.G.
STRICTLY EMBARGOED UNTIL 00.01 FRIDAY 15 JUNE

TITLE: E.G.
CAMPAIGNERS' VICTORY AS GOVERNMENT ACTS TO MAKE 'UPSKIRTING' A SPECIFIC OFFENCE

BULLET POINTS OF THE STORY: Here you want to add the three main points of the release so that the reader gets the thrust and angle of the piece straight away. E.g.

- *Government moves to make 'upskirting' a specific criminal offence*
- *Worst perpetrators set to face two years in prison*
- *Ministers demand the most serious offenders are placed on the sex offenders register*

INFORMATION: Here, you want to add the story that you want the media to run. Include relevant information that they will need here and, to give them a sense of how the story would read, you want to write it as if it was in the press already. E.g.

'Upskirting' is set to become a specific criminal offence, with perpetrators facing up to two years behind bars, under a new law backed by government.

The highly intrusive practice – colloquially known as 'upskirting' – typically involves offenders taking a picture under a person's clothing without them knowing, with the intention of viewing their genitals or buttocks.

Currently, this behaviour is being successfully prosecuted under the offence of Outraging Public Decency. However, ministers have decided to act after concerns were raised that potentially not all instances of 'upskirting' are covered by existing criminal law.

In April, the Justice Secretary David Gauke committed to ensuring the law was fit for purpose. Today, ministers have confirmed that the government will support legislation to close any potential loopholes, in order to better protect victims and increase convictions.

If your press release is about an event or happening remember to add this info in here:

WHEN:
WHERE:
TIME:

QUOTES: Here, you want quotes from only the most relevant people, and have them clearly labelled. E.g. *'Justice Minister Lucy Frazer said: [insert quote]. Lead campaigner and up skirting victim Gina Martin was overjoyed stating [insert quote]. Ryan Whelan, her lawyer, said [insert quote] and women's right's charity owner [name] reacted to this news by stating [insert quote]*

Clearly state where the press release ends by saying:

ENDS

Notes
Add any additional notes here that you think would help them tell the story correctly, or anything you think they could want to know (you don't want multiple emails asking the same questions!). Feel free to include references for research, stats or contact information in here. E.g.

- *The next stages of this bill are due to happen [insert date]*
- *You can find the bill [here]*

Once you're happy with your release, you're going to need to send it out and get it to the right people. Follow these steps to ensure your release is going to the right places. It's true that if you get a good amount of publicity – say you end up in *The Times* or on the *HuffPost* website – your story will grow a little itself and others will pick it up, but if you're looking for good coverage and general awareness, send it to anyone relevant. If you need to be more strategic with your media choices, just send to those, and if it doesn't get picked up, then go to your second choices. Make sure you consider the following things:

1. Is this the time to send a press release? If there are one or two major news stories taking over the channels (Hi, Brexit), or one theme is dominating the industry you're targeting, consider sending it at a different time. For example, if your press release is about a line of charity T-shirts, you don't want to send it during Fashion Week. Equally, if there's a date of note coming up that could benefit you, send your release with plenty of time to be featured on that relevant date – two to three weeks should do it for offline content, online has a much quicker lead period.
2. Don't send on a Sunday. It'll get pushed to the back before they've even got to their desks.
3. Look at the content of the press release – what *type* of story is this?
   - General news (the most common type, which is a newsworthy story that will

hopefully generate traditional coverage online or offline)

- Launch press release (telling people about the release of a new company, product, website, initiative, etc.)
- Event press release (telling people about an event! Make sure the 'where, who, when' is super clear here so they can communicate it, and don't write this press release in prose – try bullet points instead to get all the info across clearly)
- Product press release (a little like the launch press release, as you are showing the world something new, but this should detail the product specifications and sell the 'press angle' of the product well)

4. Based on your answers above, consider which publications, websites and newsletters your story should go in, and make a simple spreadsheet with your 'ideal names', 'good names', and 'nice to haves'. These could include journalists, editors, commissioning editors, influencers, bloggers and bookers. It all depends on the content of your release. This is your Media Contact List going forward, though, so keep it safe so you can add to it.

5. Get on Twitter, LinkedIn, PRMax, Gorkana (a media database that you have to pay for), good old Google and The Dots and get digging! To find useful contacts make sure you:

- Head to the landing pages of major publications and scroll to the bottom of the page, 'contact' will usually be small or hard to find, but through that you can often find email addresses.
- Read the masthead of any magazines you think would like to feature your story – this could be supplements (*Sunday Times Style*), glossies (*GQ*) or monthlies (*Time* magazine). The masthead is one of the first pages and will detail the names of who works there along with their job titles.
- If your story lends itself to traditional news and media, email all the major news desks. You can find their emails publicly available online. These are the departments of a newspaper or a broadcasting organisation responsible for collating the news and prepping it for publication or broadcast. Often, emailing news desks means you'll get a response from someone in the department and that's a great contact to have. Generally, you want to take note of who responds to you and what their role is, in case they're happy to help you in the future.

9

YOU AND THE MEDIA

*6 Whoever controls the media, controls
the mind.9*

Jim Morrison

O kay, so a fairly dramatic quote to start this chapter,
but it's true: how you communicate to these people
informs how they feel about your work and what actions they
take. Traditional media is still such a powerful force when
it comes to connecting with the masses, and whether it's a
national TV channel or a local newspaper, you want to consider each one's merits and how they could aid your message,
because the media should support your overall strategy, not
come first. Make sure you're fitting it around your aim, not
doing it because it's 'exciting' – even if that may be hard.

At the beginning of my campaign, I was trying to

educate as many people as possible on the shocking fact that upskirting was not a sexual offence in England and Wales, and traditional daytime TV was a great way for me to do that. However, your cause might not be as unknown as mine was, so you might look to other forms of media to help you – each campaign, and therefore each media strategy, is as individual as the activist doing it!

Generally, editors, producers and bookers aren't going to approach you for your story, unless you've made some real noise on social media first, but if you pitch your work and your cause in the right way, they're likely to feature your story.

GETTING MEDIA COVERAGE

I was lucky when starting my campaign because I knew a few people (vaguely) at a couple of women's websites. But if you're starting this totally afresh and your campaign's something that deals with your local community, it's a no-brainer to start with local radio, newspaper and TV stations. And actually, even if it's not, that could be a good move anyway as local media generally have bigger connections: for example, your local BBC station is linked to the bigger BBC network, and it means your issue will be on their agenda, you'll have your foot in the door, and your details will be on file for the entire network so they can call you back or get in touch if they hear of something they'd like you to comment on, or if there's an update on your campaign.

Here are a few tips on how to get in touch with your local news channels and newspapers:

- Do a little research and find out which shows or publications deal with which issues and what their agendas usually are.
- Use their website to look at the producers on each show or the news editors of each paper (then do a sneaky LinkedIn search to make sure it's them!).
- Type keywords into the Twitter search bar to find people who work at different stations, news channels and newspapers. Generally they'll have their place of work in their bio, which Twitter will pick up on, and lots of them set their DMs to 'open' for new stories.
- Corroborate your stalking findings on LinkedIn or through picking up a copy of your local paper and reading through the by-lines and info at the front.

Another great option is to approach websites that deal with similar issues or issues related to what you're talking about. For example, at the beginning of my campaign I picked Refinery29 as my partner to run an editorial series with, as they were often looking for human stories and in particular stories focusing on women's issues. If you look to work with someone who has a good reach, is relevant to your cause but isn't unrealistic at first, you're amplifying your story by a few realistic steps, which will allow you to then go to bigger websites or publications from there with some authority behind you. Build it up cleverly. You could also approach freelance journalists who write on related content. To do this, search editorial websites for similar pieces and take a note of the name of the writer or journalist, then – you guessed it – get on Twitter. This is a great example of when it's best to let someone else do the talking. That journalist already has an authoritative voice, network and reach that you may not, so work with them and then let them write up the piece. If you're concerned about specifics, you can ask for copy sign-off from them or for them to read it back to you to make sure.

Tip: On social media platforms check if their email is in their bio, and if not, slide into their DMs to pique their interest, e.g. 'I have a story I think you may be interested in and would love to chat about it! Could I drop you an email? Thanks!'

Finding and getting in touch with the right contacts is only half the battle, because now you need to pitch them something that they can't wait to use. This is an odd process at first, though. It always feels like a bit of a weird one for campaigners: we're so used to speaking from the heart that sometimes it feels odd to start selling your campaign as if it's a commodity, but you need to convince them that this is an interesting story that people want to hear, and to do that you need to present it in a way that's valuable to them.

When writing your pitch email try and keep it to around 200 words – these are busy people and they get a lot of pitches in their inbox. Feel free to head back to chapter 7 and use your elevator pitch for this, but make sure you catch their attention first by adding:

- A quick sentence on a related story they covered a while ago as evidence as to why you think the following could work well for them.
- Mention that this is an exclusive look at this campaign for either local radio, TV or a local newspaper (it doesn't have to be a complete exclusive, but if it is for this type of media, tell them that).
- Tie it into a wider cultural story, e.g. my campaign was often linked to #MeToo, which at the beginning made it relevant and pricked reporters' ears.
- Use a bold headline for your campaign so they can picture the story, e.g. *Victim of upskirting fights back and is trying to change the law.*

If you can sell your campaign and its message in an interesting way that's relevant to that particular channel and the news landscape at the time, you're on to a winner! Feel free to invite local press along to any events or initiatives you're holding too, so they can report on the campaign generally, but always give them at least a few weeks' notice!

This may come as a shock, but

the old adage 'no publicity is bad publicity' has no place in activism. Activism is all about optics.

CHOOSING THE OPPORTUNITY FOR A REASON

Carefully chosen media can do amazing things for your campaign and can really push it in the direction you need, so you need to be thinking about what channels are best for you and why. Take a look at your timeline, work out what kind of media you'll need for each objective, and ask some questions:

- Is this the right channel for this message, or could it be more impactful or better digested elsewhere?
- Do I need to do this media myself or could this be communicated better by or with someone else?
- What audience does this media outlet have? Why am I specifically targeting them? And why now?

That last question is, in my opinion, the most critical. Of course there may be a period of time when you need to do as much media as possible to get as many people on board, but if you're no longer in that stage, you should only really do *the right* media, to reach *the right* audience. A good test is that if you can't pinpoint why you're doing this media and want to speak to this specific audience, you shouldn't be doing it.

Remember: If you are doing media and want your Gatekeepers to see it, consider what media would make their ears prick up the most. What names – when mentioned in a media briefing to them – would make them take notice? If there is a money-related aspect to your campaign, could you get the Financial Times *to run something? If you're working on something to do with the environment, could* National Geographic *be an ideal hit? We had pieces across major newspapers, including pieces written by Ryan in the* Spectator, *because we knew that would interest MPs. The Refinery29 partnership at the beginning was about activating young women. You can see the strategy here, and as we all know, it has to remain strategic.*

TIMING IS EVERYTHING

Timing is a bloody nebulous thing, so to make this one easier, plot your ideas for media on your timeline. You don't have to know exactly which specific channels or type of media you are doing, you can just detail the type of media that would help whatever you're trying to push at that time. For instance, you could plot 'local media to gain awareness', or 'media including debates to make the point about ____ clear', or 'editorial pieces in places Gatekeepers will see them'. That way you have a general outline of what media will fit with your strategy and you can refer to that as you go. Generally, media is great for putting pressure on companies, people or your Gatekeepers. But it only works if people are still interested, so remember to have 'media blackouts' when media isn't absolutely necessary. If you continue trying to tell the same story for weeks at a time the public will get bored. Over the course of my eighteen-month campaign, I probably popped back up in the news, guns blazing, about four or five times. The 'blackouts' in-between gave people time to forget me, so that when I came back with an update they wondered where the story had now got to and were engaged.

Give people time to miss you so they can recognise what progress has been made.

Use the media when you need it, not only when you get offered it.

CONTROLLING THE STORY (AND ANGLE)

Media can be daunting, and each media outlet will want to focus on a different bit of the story or take a certain 'angle' with the information you've given them. You could be trying to draw attention to specific statistics and they'd rather bring up an inflammatory story that barely relates. Your job is to keep the conversation on track and control the narrative. This isn't easy to do and is probably what I found most challenging when I began to do media. The main trick is that when you are asked something that could steer you off message, don't feed the interviewer by giving them an answer that'll allow that conversation to continue. You want to give them enough so that you don't seem rude, but then steer the conversation back to what you want to talk about. The best way to do this is to find something in their question that relates to your message or could be applied to what you want to talk about. Here's an example from an interview I did:

Interviewer: *The fight for women's rights has taken on new life in the last year, but a lot of people are saying #MeToo hasn't done enough – do you think #MeToo has really worked?*

Me: *It definitely has taken on a new lease of life, and there's a reason. Women are done with brushing things off and putting up with assault. That's why this campaign is so important to me, and to so many people, including police commissioners. It's a chance for our government to address a form of sexual harassment and set an example, and set the precedent that upskirting is wrong.*

You can see, pretty clearly, that the interviewer wanted to get into a debate on the #MeToo movement more than they wanted to talk to me about my campaign. Did I want to answer the question about #MeToo and say HELL YES IT'S WORKED WHAT ARE YOU TALKING ABOUT, DAVID? Sure. But at this point in my campaign, I needed to get a certain message out there. Avoiding the questions will make you feel very weird, but it's just one of the tactics you'll have to employ when controlling the story. The golden rule, above all, is this:

Don't give them all the information they want. Give them only the information you want them to have.

DOING LIVE TV

If you're doing live TV or being interviewed, the first few times can feel very weird, so here are some tips I've picked up along the way:

- Wear something that a mic pack can easily clip onto. I once wore a thin dress for *This Morning* and had to pull my skirt up around my waist as the mic guy attached it to my tights. He asked 'What are you on for today?' I replied, '... Upskirting.' We both laughed. A lot.
- Don't wear a mad pattern. It goes absolutely mental on the monitors.
- Do not be late – it's live!
- You're not expected to find your own way; you'll be given a pass and collected by a runner from the foyer.
- Leave your bags in the green room instead of carting them into the manic studio like I once did.
- You'll probably be silently plopped into a chair by a producer while the cameras are rolling and are focused on the presenter, just sit quietly and watch them finish their link.
- Once you're on set, you have no idea what cameras are on you, but be aware that there are cameras everywhere. Sometimes there'll be screens of YOUR OWN FACE on the desk you're sitting

at – don't look at them even though, my god, you want to. Lock your eyes on the presenter and do not look anywhere else.

- You shouldn't be expected to get to and from the studio by yourself if you don't live near it – especially if you're not being paid. If you're a guest on the show it's totally normal to ask for a car to get you there. They have a budget and they will book a taxi for you.
- You don't necessarily have to be in the city the show's studios are in – if you can't get there, ask if they could do a live link from a local studio, or a pre-record.

DOING EDITORIAL INTERVIEWS

Here are some quick tips for these:

- Do not expect journalists to tell you what kind of piece they're writing and what it will entail – they almost never do. It's up to you to ask questions.
- Ask them, upfront, who else will be featured in the piece and who will be quoted. The amount of interviews I've done where I've been quoted next to someone I totally disagree with and it sounded like we were in the same room is mad. It didn't look good for me to be associated with that person at that time so I should have asked first. Don't be

afraid of backing out of a piece if you don't agree with it, or who's involved. There will be others.

- Ask them what the angle of the piece is.
  This is key.
- If you're doing phone interviews, ask them to specifically state when you're 'on record'. You'd think they would do this anyway but many of them expect you to know.
- If there's anything you don't want them to put in, caveat it by telling them it's 'off the record'.
- Don't be too shy to go back to the journalist and ask them not to include something if you think you said something out of place or something unhelpful to your campaign. I committed an absolute blinder once before. I assumed it would be off the record, and it wasn't. I can't even bring myself to write it here, that's how bad it was. And it was in print.
- If the piece is online, don't be scared of correcting a mistake they've made or asking them to take something out. Just explain and be friendly.

ON THE RADIO

- Take your chewing gum out!
- Keep relatively still so the levels don't jump around. If you're moving and gesturing they're going to hear it all.

- Loads of radio stations will want you to do a call in. They'll call and you'll be almost immediately put through to the show – sometimes I've received phone calls and all I can hear are radio ads, and that's how I know I'm on the radio. It's up to you to listen for the presenter to introduce you.
- Phone-ins are always so much clearer on FaceTime than over a mobile, so if you can do it on FaceTime offer to do that – it also means you won't have signal issues.
- As your interview winds down, the presenter will often say thank you and go on to the next link without giving you a chance to say goodbye. Watch out for this, or you'll do what I did and say 'Okay byeeeeeee' over them introducing the next segment. Smooth.

Whatever type of media you do, be passionate, stay on message, *give away only what is valuable to the campaign at that time* and follow up afterwards by interacting with anyone talking about your interview or work online. Social media ignites conversations about TV, radio and editorial content, so comment on, share and like messages from whoever is supporting your work. After all, that kind of support is what will get you to the end goal.

10

ADVOCACY

advocacy
/ˈadvəkəsi/
noun
1. Public support for or recommendation of a particular cause or policy.

S o, now you feel like you have a good amount of information out there about your campaign, but you want to take it up a notch. You need to encourage those who have heard of your work to be proactive on your behalf. You want to get to hard-to-reach people and have them be part of your army. This section is all about getting actual tangible support from people in order to drive your issue home to your Gatekeepers.

GETTING THE PUBLIC TO TAKE ACTION

Public pressure is powerful, but if people have only heard of your campaign and aren't actively engaged, they're unlikely to help you push forward. This is where advocacy comes in. If you've laid the groundwork right, your awareness campaign will have got people emotionally engaged and now they'll be ready to pitch in. Worst-case scenario? They didn't see your awareness campaign, but we are now living in a time when people want to feel as if they're doing something to help. They're looking for the opportunity to take action, so more often than not, they will. Here are some ways you can ask the public to help:

Enlist the public to put pressure on your Gatekeepers

The public can help you put pressure on, or bring issues to, powerful people, but never – and I repeat – never give out someone's email address (even if it's public property) or directly 'target' them. You don't want to annoy this person and fill up their inbox – they're there to help you. You want them to be swayed, not forced, into making change. Forcefulness often just results in your Gatekeeper not wanting anything to do with you – and we want to work *with* them, not make their lives hell! Twitter is a great tool for showing them the public's passion because notifications won't be too annoying for them, but it'll get the issue on their agenda. Remember, though, you need to set the tone.

Tweet something diplomatic that asks a question or invites your Gatekeeper to meet with you, and encourage people to retweet it. I used my petition functionality to send automated emails to Members of Parliament imploring them to act. It put the pressure on, sure, but it wasn't combative or forceful. Yes, they may have had anywhere between five and twenty professionally written emails over a period of time, but that's as bad as it got. I didn't create a URL of their name or encourage people to constantly go after them on Twitter.

In short, be persistent but don't become a problem for them.

Ask people to support, and shout about, updates in your campaign

Have a centralised point for people to come to in order to keep up with your work. As we've discussed, you don't need to necessarily build a website – your personal social feeds are good enough!

When you need to put some extra pressure on a company, a person or a decision-maker you're working with, use the public much like you would the media. But remember, you only get a handful of opportunities. People don't want to be asked continually to do things and their passion isn't an inexhaustible resource for you. Using my petition, I could update all signees with checkpoints in my campaign or difficulties that they could help me with, but I did it rarely – only when there was something big. Feel free to use your social feeds to update people, or go for something more traditional like an email update. But remember, you want any data collection to be above board, and this is where a petition is really helpful; you can use the database of your signees to send them updates or ask them to complete an action for you! Remember though, whatever you ask them to do, make it clear exactly what you're asking, exactly why, and remove as many steps from the process for them as you can. You want to make any action as easy as humanly possible so that more people are likely to do it.

Examples of ways in which people could help could be:

- Sharing the campaign with friends or family
- Writing to, or emailing, designated people and asking for a specific action
- Signing a petition
- Recording a short video or taking a photo for you (think of the #smearforsmear campaign – could they hold up a sign or create something with visual recognition?)
- Show their support at an event, march or rally

Remember: There are enough unemotional robots and corporate kings in this world. If you're fighting for something, let people in on the reality of it – I mean, don't spend every day telling people you have no idea what you're doing or how scared you are (you still need people to buy into your idea and think you can pull it off!), but allow them to see the journey and feel part of it. Show

BE PERSISTENT

them what it's like and take them along with you. I know I feel way more involved in a campaign if I care about the person behind it. Campaigns don't have to be corporate when talking to the public. Being real is what makes people stay with you.

GETTING PEOPLE WITH POWER TO BACK YOU

There is one type of person who could garner invaluable support for you if you could get them on board: someone with notability. Unlike fame, notability applies to anyone who is notable for their work, so this could include individuals who are high up or well known in their industry, and sure, of course this also includes celebrities and other people of note, too. And collaborating with such people is a big one, because fame is a strange beast that has the ability to engage the public and the elite at the same time – even the most powerful people can get star-struck and will pay attention to a big name they love!

The ideal kind of advocacy is a group of 'ambassadors' that span different industries and worlds; this gives your campaign more breadth and credibility across multiple conversations. Here, we're to play a game not unlike the old 'Who Would Be Your Dream Dinner Guests?', but instead we'll be creating your ideal group of advocates: the kind of people that, if they shouted about your cause, could get your campaign recognition that would open doors and get you into the room with those who could make it happen.

Please note, though, that unlike the dinner party game all your dream people have to be alive, otherwise my god that's a terrifying and useless list of advocates.

Tip: Before we start building our team, it's critical you get ready to ask yourself: why them? You really don't want to pick people because of how many followers they have. You want to pick people whose values closely align with your campaign's values, or those who care about or have experienced what you're working to change.

First, write a list of different types of notable people:

- Influencers (bloggers, writers, social media personalities, etc.)
- Celebrities (actors, singers, athletes, presenters, models, etc.)
- Journalists (editors, writers, reporters, columnists, etc.)
- Academics (educators, social critics, political commentators, academic writers, etc.)
- Creatives (photographers, poets, designers, painters, illustrators, etc.)
- Community authorities (police commissioners, politicians, council workers, etc.)
- Charity founders, ambassadors or fellow activists

Try to populate this list with as many names as you can think of who would be interested in your cause. Make sure there's something solid that links them to it, though. For example, Leonardo DiCaprio would be great for a campaign on climate change, and the activist Simon Hooper

(@fatherofdaughters) would be a good fit for a campaign about paternity leave. Get out the list of themes you wrote in the 'Getting your campaign to the right people' section in Chapter 8 and have a look at those groups – have any people of note talked about those things? Is there anyone who seems a perfect fit for your work? Have you already talked to or had contact with some of these people in the Awareness section (Chapter 7)? Maybe it's time to utilise those contacts now!

If you get stuck, try these tips:

- Have a look at charities that deal with a topic related to your campaign and scan through who their ambassadors have been.
- Search news and journalism websites (the BBC, *Guardian, Telegraph*) to find articles relating to your campaign topic using keywords. Read the articles and jot down any names. Look these people up and see if they have any weight in the field they are in.
- Google sensationalist headline phrases and wait for Google to fill in the names for you. For example, I used 'speaks out on upskirt photos', 'calls out photographers for upskirt photos', 'paparazzi take knicker shots of', etc.
- Search key phrases in Twitter and look at the 'top tweets'. Any story with a notable person at the heart of it will get more engagement and be filed into 'top tweets'.

HOW TO GET ACCESS TO PEOPLE

Once you've got a list of people from different levels and industries, compile five people from the five most relevant industries or arenas and begin looking for their contact details. For anyone outside of that 'untouchable' fame circle, you should be able to find an email for them or their office fairly easily, either through their social media bios or by digging deep on Google, but for anyone famous, yes, it's a little trickier. And I know what you're thinking: 'Leonardo DiCaprio doesn't just have his email on Google, Gina.' No, you're right, he doesn't. But generally, if you look hard enough you will be able to find an agency or publicist contact for his team, and, again, if you sell your cause effectively they may forward it to him. That's exactly what happened to me with Holly Willoughby, and that's how she became an advocate of the campaign. In direct contrast, with Dermot O'Leary I was sat in a cafe with a friend when he walked in wearing a bike helmet, and suddenly a pigeon flew into his head. I shouted 'Whoa!', at which point he took off the bike helmet, and I exclaimed ' . . . and it's *you*!' We had a laugh, I messaged him later that day saying 'Hope the pigeon's okay', and then he became a supporter of the campaign. I wouldn't say that's a watertight strategy, but messaging people is always a good shout!

In terms of getting in touch with 'famous' people, you need to know exactly what you want from them, and why, before you even begin to try to contact them. These people are generally unspeakably busy, so you need to make sure that what you're asking them to do is something that requires little to no effort, otherwise they're not going to do it.

When asking powerful people to back you, the rule is: what is the simplest thing they could do that would have the biggest positive impact on your campaign?

Generally an easy answer to this is a social media post, because it:

- Shows their support in no uncertain terms
- Allows you to get a particular message out on a huge scale
- Comes directly from them so has more gravitas
- Helps to raise your social profile so you can speak to more people

When you contact someone's publicist or office, you want them to know what you're asking within the first email, so that if they're in a good mood they can just forward it on to the person you're trying to contact. For example, if you float the idea of this person doing a social post in support of you, but don't actually give them the template for the post, it means they have to get back in touch and ask questions, and they probably won't have time for that, or will forget. So, let's imagine you're asking for a tweet. When you email, supply them with:

1. A brief introduction to yourself
2. A brief elevator pitch
3. Why this is relevant to their client/how their client has already shown they care about this or something closely related
4. What you're asking for (a tweet)

Then, as we've previously discussed, write out the tweet for them, and don't feel weird about it. Trust me, they'll be stoked you've done it for them. To write the perfect promo tweet, keep these points in mind:

- Remember to write it to 280 characters. They will probably copy and paste it so fast they won't even look, so make sure it fits!
- Include your hashtag and your handle (and *triple* check that they're right!).
- Include an image as pictures always get more engagement (attach this to the email) and be super clear that you want it to be attached to the tweet.
- Look at their previous social posts and ensure you're writing it in their tone of voice, not yours. Keep it general (don't do an impression of them!) but make sure you are writing it in a way that could work on their feed.
- Make it clear that they are 'free to use this tweet', or to use it as a template, but to please include all handles and hashtags.

As you make your way down your list, think about and work out what you're asking of your other ideal advocates, i.e. your academics, community authorities and journalists. Do you need them to help with awareness or prepping something for the action stage? Are you asking a columnist you think is relevant to feature your campaign if it fits into their writing? Are you asking academics to corroborate your potential solution to a problem, and if so, does that mean you'd like them to sign an unofficial document in support of it? Are you asking a local artist to collaborate with you on their next mural or fashion line? Are you asking a police commissioner to give you a quote you can add to your press release? If we take the examples I've given above and think about them in terms of a campaign time-line, we can see where those ideas would fit best.

1. Asking a columnist you think is relevant to feature your campaign if it fits into their writing.
This fits well under awareness, and getting your message out to the right audiences.

2. Are you asking academics to corroborate your potential solution to a problem, and if so, does that mean you'd like them to sign an unofficial document in support of it?
This is advocacy but it fits under action too because it's not support for support's sake. This is you building authority behind you that demonstrates your solution is supported by those who know the most about it. As a general rule, there might be crossover when it comes to your Three 'A's, and that's okay. Steps may need to be

repeated, or parts of one section may naturally fit into parts of the next, and that's also okay. Like everything in life, this process isn't always linear.

3. Are you asking a local artist to collaborate with you on their next mural or fashion line?
This fits well under awareness, and getting your message out to the right audiences.

4. Are you asking a police commissioner to give you a quote you can add to your press release?
This fits under advocacy but could take place during any stage of your campaign – it could be in the action stage, too.

The possibilities are endless, but it's all about working out *where that person can bring the most value to your strategy,* and being open and honest with them about how they could use their platform for the greater good and help you achieve your goal. And remember, don't feel guilty for enlisting their help. It's good for them to be associated with a grassroots cause, and even though you may feel pushy at times, you're doing this for the greater good.

PETITIONS FOR ADVOCACY

As we've discussed, a petition is an amazing tool, and this is especially true for advocacy, because it's pretty much a list of names and signatures that show popular support for a cause. To me, they are a given because they require completely minimal effort from the signees, but have maximum impact if they grow big enough and are used in an effective way. If you can gain popular support for or against an issue, why wouldn't you? As with so much of campaigning, petitions are about timing, too. Start one when you feel there is at least a little bit of interest about your issue, because my god when you're trying to push for change, there's nothing that makes your stomach sink more than a petition that's struggling to get support, and getting no signees is a visual representation of that. Much like crowdfunding, people often only hear about or want to sign petitions that have some momentum, so that they feel part of a movement. If yours is dragging along and then stalls just above 100 signatures, it's going to be a job in itself getting it going again, so make sure you get people interested in your issue beforehand either online or by holding events, meetings, workshops or more casual meet-ups and discussions.

Another important part of ensuring your petition works is making sure it's a clear part of your overall strategy. Don't treat it as an add-on. Make it a clear objective for you and your supporters. As with all activism, there are always multiple streams of work happening at any one time, but you want the people supporting you to feel clear about what they need to do to help and when, so when you put the petition out, make sure it's the main focus.

When starting your petition try and:

1. Make sure it has a short and attention-grabbing headline *that clearly communicates the issue.* For the original petition that brought upskirting to attention and the public eye, my title was:

I had upskirt photos taken of me – sign to make this a sexual offence in England & Wales!

For my petition that automatically sent emails to MPs asking them to change the law, the title was:

Sign to email your MP: Make upskirt photos a specific sexual offence!

I realise this isn't rocket science, but it's an important lesson in clarity and getting to the point. You'll notice how for my original petition, I positioned the human story at the beginning, then I finished with the objective of the campaign. It worked because the human element was intriguing and clickbait-y, but it also showed exactly what their signature would help me do.

2. Tell people in the first paragraph why they should sign. Even better if you can do it in the first two sentences. People are busy and they're used to consuming content quickly. For a video, you need to catch people's attention in the first two seconds, but in writing it is far harder as it takes longer to read than to consume images. So, it's up to you to write a compelling story and get them involved. Remember

what I said earlier about the importance of human stories.
I started with my story because I knew the human story
would work, but if you don't have any personal experience,
remember there's nothing stopping you from working with
someone who's been affected by the issue you're fighting for
and writing it up with them. However, if it's not something
you've experienced, it's not your story to tell. Remember
that. Get creative, but as a general rule keep the most
interesting part near the front. Quickly follow it with what
the problem is and finish with what needs to be done and
how to solve it. Remember to make it clear why you are so
passionate about the issue (as passion is infectious!) and try
to make an emotional connection with the reader. Here's
the intro from my petition as an example.

*Last week at British Summer Time music festival in London, two
men were taking upskirt photos of my – you know what I mean –
without me knowing. They sent them to each other and I saw it
on one guy's phone. I grabbed his phone and ran to security, who
called the police. After looking at the photos, confirming it was me,
and questioning him, the Met Police told me, 'There's not much we
can do.' Upskirting is not a sexual offence. Sign here to show MPs
they should make it one. It could mean we change the law together.*

11

READY, SET, ACTION

action
/ˈakʃ(ə)n/
noun
The fact or process of doing something, typically to achieve an aim.

A h, yes. This is where you fly the toolkit coop, my friends. If you've completed the awareness and advocacy stage, only you know what action is required now. To be honest, calling this stage 'action' actually seems insanely reductive, because it can be pretty complex. It's effectively where you take the awareness and advocacy you've worked so hard to get and use it to strategically work towards the end goal. This stage might take you months, or years, and you'll probably have to repeat the first two stages in different ways, in different arenas, but if you're moving the campaign forward, pushing through barriers, making stuff happen and taking one step forward (regardless of whether sometimes you must take two steps back) then you're in the action stage. It's where you'll be entering the spaces that could lead to your objective, rather than educating those outside of them.

THE POLITICS OF ACTIVISM

As we've previously discussed, politics isn't just about Westminster. Politics pertains to almost everything to do with people, power and how these intersect. Most spaces are political: your office, your classroom, your friendship groups often. In this section I want to touch on some of the scenarios in which politics is at play and hopefully then you'll be able to recognise it and navigate it better.

Handling high-pressure meetings

The word 'meetings' throws up a whole load of terrifying imagery for a lot of us. Especially for women. What if you say the wrong thing? What if you don't know the answer to a question? If you're anything like me, you always feel like the 'little guy' in meetings: the person across the table is more important than you, has more to say than you, and you feel like you're on the back foot. Lack of confidence, or, in the worst-case scenario, Impostor syndrome – a psychological pattern in which an individual doubts their accomplishments and has a persistent internalised fear of being exposed as a 'fraud' – can be so bloody hard to overcome, and it can actually inhibit you from doing your best work. In activism, Impostor syndrome is rife, as you're often operating in uncharted territory and spaces of power where you may not feel entirely comfortable. But there is actually something that can banish the nerves that come with high-pressure meetings: going to them. Finding them scary is tough, but the only way out is through. The only way to cure fear is action – to prove to yourself that you can do it. That's it. So, with that in mind, here are my tips for getting yourself in the room and getting on with it:

Be prepared
Benjamin Franklin once said that by 'failing to prepare, you are preparing to fail', and I can't believe how much that rang true during my campaigning. Don't go hard on yourself, though. Just make sure you're crystal clear on who you're meeting and why, what you need to get out of this meeting, what you think their objective is going to be, and what the agenda for the meeting is. If you know that information and you have your elevator pitch prepared, you're pretty prepped and that makes for a far more confident version of yourself walking through that door.

Don't delay
If this meeting needs to happen, do it now. Don't wait until you're 'more prepared' or put it off. All that does is give fear time to fester and doubts time to grow.

Avoid caffeine or stimulants

It's so easy to think that downing a flat white before you go into a big meeting will make you far more alert and 'on it', but in reality all it will do will make it harder for you to stay grounded and calm. Ditch it.

Remember why you're there

You have been invited to this meeting for a reason. You didn't fall over and end up in that room, you were asked to be there. Your presence there was important enough that the person you're scared of agreed to meet with you. Remember that. This is not a fluke.

Create an alter ego

If Beyoncé needs an alter ego then we're allowed one too, okay? Imagine a version of you who isn't nervous or insecure. Picture them in your head, walking into the office, knowing they should be there. Give them a name, and when you get ready for this important meeting, wear what they would wear. Listen to empowering music to pep you up. Play that role as if your life depends on it.

Body language

You can half-convince yourself of your own ability by keeping an eye on your body language. Make sure you walk in with your shoulders back and chin up. Speak clearly, slowly and with volume – don't whisper or mumble. Sit upright in your chair. Clasp your hands on your knees firmly. And, above everything else, maintain eye contact. Even if it's bloody painful. Eye contact is a game-changer, and if you can't maintain it, people may struggle to believe you have the tools to make big things happen. Force yourself to look at their eyes when you talk, and when they talk to you.

Your job here is sort of to fake it until you make it. By that I mean *act as if you're confident* even when you feel like a gibbering wreck. I've been told multiple times that I always seem 'so self-assured', but the truth is, I'm often totally freaking out inside – I've just mastered the ability to hide it and project confidence. I can be convincing even when I'm not sure that I am, and I've only really noticed it when I've watched myself back. The last two years of pretending to be bold and brave has got me through meetings and high-pressure situations, and some time this year I looked back and realised that whether I'd successfully navigated those nerve-wracking moments through genuine confidence or faking it, it didn't matter. I'd got through them regardless, and that was enough to make me believe in myself a little more. I'd inadvertently convinced *myself.* So go in there, do your best, and remember that in so many other meetings that went before, it wasn't your project. But this is. This is *yours.* You started it. You know it better than anyone and the ball is in your court here. Go and do you.

BECOMING VALUABLE TO YOUR GATEKEEPERS

Your relationship with your Gatekeepers is a complex one. They can't tell you everything – they have priorities, they are part of a business and it's not going to be as easy as meeting them, discussing the issue, agreeing and then changing whatever you set out to change – believe me. But, that doesn't mean you can't have a productive and successful working relationship with them. There has to be a certain level of trust there and there has to be a commitment from both sides. It may take you time to get that, but if you are strategic and do things right, you'll get there. Often with campaigning it can feel like David and Goliath all over again – you can feel small and insignificant. But the truth is, you are a valuable part of this partnership too and there are ways you can make sure you're not just some person with an idea who wandered in one day and never quite got any further.

Be passionate, switched on and convincing

This comes from taking the time upfront to know your campaign, the social landscape you're working in and your beliefs before you get into these types of meetings. The chances are, by the time you've got to this stage you will have gained a level of confidence you didn't have at the start and you will definitely know your campaign and issue inside out. Remember, though, that when you're here you do have the opportunity to be the type of person your Gatekeeper wants to be associated with. Powerful people are fully aware that trust is fragile with the general public, or that their company needs some good press, and you can help them with that. Know your worth, as they know theirs.

268

Do your research and know your shit

You want them to know you're serious and you want them to trust you. The partnership can only work if there's genuine trust there. First impressions are critical, and if you walk in that room and don't know what you're talking about, what you're asking for or what your campaign's really about, then, quite frankly, you're DOA. But I'm not talking nerves here, I'm talking about the fundamental information your campaign rests on. You don't need to know absolutely every single answer to every single question – especially if you've split skillsets between a couple of you, or a team. With my campaign, I didn't know the ins and outs of the legislation, and I was very clear that that was Ryan's remit, but my remit? I knew what I was talking about. I had put the work in beforehand.

Do not, under any circumstances, go to them for the solution

Take the time beforehand – whether that's months or even years – to do all of the heavy-lifting before you get anywhere near meeting with your Gatekeeper. If you walk into a meeting, present a problem to them, show them the statistics and then ask them what they're going to do about it, you should show yourself outside. The entire point of being a campaigner is coming up with solutions to problems, and they don't need someone to add to the list of things they have to solve. Do every single thing possible to make this as easy as you can for them. When we headed into Parliament, we had already written legislation options, had had them sense-checked and received endorsement from the best law authorities in the country. All we were asking was for MPs to support the piece of paper in front of them and take action, nothing more.

Us 'regular people' have a propensity to get angry about stuff and then demand someone else solve it, but as an activist that is your job.

So do as much of the hard work as you can for them. This can mean:

1. *Giving them something they can't find elsewhere.*
Collect data on the issue that you can't find anywhere else. Surveys, interviews and conducting research can really help you in the long run – especially if you're dealing with a little-known problem. Arming them with new information can make you pretty valuable to them. Could you confidentially collect the human stories in a spreadsheet and store them for safe-keeping? I collated hundreds of stories from women who had been upskirted to encourage the government's decision to support us, because there just wasn't enough research on the issue in general. I came to them with something they didn't already have, and something that helped them prove to others that supporting me was the right decision. Remember, though, if you're collecting any information

or data from people, it's best to use a tool to do so to keep everything official. For instance, I asked people if they would be comfortable to provide a story of their experience, then I detailed how it would be used. A survey or petition is a good tool for this. Encouraging people to share their stories in the petition comments is helpful or using a survey tool like typeform.com to collect data works well too.

2. *Coming up with multiple solutions to the problem, not just one.* If there is space to change what you're trying to change with a few different approaches, explore them all and present them to your Gatekeeper. You don't know exactly how they'll work, and it may be the case that one solution works better for them than another, so show them you're open to options.

Keep them a priority

Your relationship with your Gatekeepers, when you have it, is critical to the success of your campaign and therefore the GOOD OF THE WORLD, PEOPLE! Don't do anything to jeopardise this. If you're still undertaking awareness work with them, keep in mind the importance of how the media, events and work you are doing makes them appear too, as they are now associated with you. Any person working with a grassroots activist knows that the campaign is number one for them, but your relationship with your Gatekeeper should be a close second. There may be times when you have to do media in order to remind your Gatekeeper that

'Hey, I'm still here and not going anywhere', and that won't be a surprise to them, either. But keeping the pressure on them to act shouldn't be to the detriment of your relationship – otherwise, what's the point in getting this far?

WORKING WITH THOSE WHOSE VIEWS DIFFER FROM YOURS

Us 'regular' people can feel disillusioned about those in power most of the time. We feel angry often. And when we feel angry, our instinct is to fight against the power structures that could have got us to this place. I understand that feeling – I think we all do. But when you make the decision to take on the 'bigger fight' and want to force real, meaningful change, you'll struggle to do that without working *inside* the power structures you have wanted to fight against previously. You need to get under the skin of a problem to solve it, and you need to get inside a power structure to have the best chance of creating change. Getting at the problem from the inside is where the real change happens. You might find you end up working closely with people whose views you don't necessarily agree with, too (obviously within reason – I'm assuming you won't be working with a dictator here). We are all so used to being in our little political bubbles online that we don't have to interact with people whose ideas of society are wildly different from ours, but when you go into this kind of work, it's likely that – at some point – you'll have to form a team with those people. I believe that's a good thing.

No one becomes a better activist by refusing to work with someone because they think differently.

We all have different perspectives and views, but the important thing is that yours and theirs intersect on this subject. Cancel culture is a big thing, and sure, it's easy to cancel someone when you don't have to interact with them, but activism requires a little more nuance, a little more diplomacy and a little more patience. It's about working with the right people, whether or not you see eye-to-eye on everything, for the greater good. Remember that.

You may also come up against people who don't help you as you'd hoped they would. In my experience, early engagement with the Ministry of Justice's Conservative ministers was disappointing. Dominic Raab, for instance, repeatedly stated that the government was looking at whether the law 'remained appropriate', but the point was that it had never been appropriate – there had always been a gap. I started to get frustrated and honestly thought I'd never get anywhere. But Ryan thought different. He made the point that the reality of being a government minister, the politics at play, meant that we needed to persuade and build momentum – with or without Raab. 'Make him a speedbump, not a roadblock.' Dominic wasn't giving me anything, so we got strategic. We didn't write off working with the 'Justice Minister'. That wouldn't have helped us, at all.

BEING CLEVER WITH THE MEDIA DURING ACTION

Ironically, the Action stage can often feel a little flatter compared with the previous two because it doesn't have the same roaring momentum they often do. With Awareness you have the excitement of a) launching, and b) people discovering your cause for the first time. With Advocacy, you get the thrill of seeing people actively support something you've worked so hard to create. With Action? Well, generally you have a lot of meetings, conversations and discussions, and most likely setbacks, too, as this is where more people become involved in the core group and it can get more complex. You'll probably be doing less with the media in order to focus on the heavy-lifting and get this thing finished. In some action phases there may be energetic stages such as a rally or a march of some kind, but as we discussed, we generally don't want it to have to get to that point, so the action part can sometimes weirdly feel quite quiet after the first two. If you feel this way, remember that this is where the real difference happens: when people don't know you're doing it. The amount of reporters who have asked me what it was like when I 'found out' upskirting had become illegal is astounding. I used to get quite annoyed and retort that I'd 'been there every step of the way, actually', but then I realised that I'd done my job right. The media weren't meant to know the behind-the-scenes of what had happened. I was too busy doing the *actual* work when I wasn't in the papers, and that's the way it should be, because a lot of the change happened quietly. In meetings, over phone calls, in writing. This silence is not only critical for reaching the finish line, but it also guarantees one thing: better media coverage when you want it. Keeping quiet and working hard means that people will be far more receptive when you have something interesting to say and want to talk. Short bursts of media are key to keeping people on board. And if you can guarantee some good press for your Gatekeeper, that's no bad thing.

WHEN CAMPAIGNING ENDS

SUCCESS

If you get to the end of your campaign and the outcome is what you'd hoped for, you may find it hard to get closure. When people tell me I've changed the law it literally feels like they've said I made a cup of tea, because ...

What you work for, however big, becomes your reality

Regardless of whether or not you feel the weight of what you've done, celebrate the progress you've pushed for. The world is starved of uplifting and exciting good news – we need more of it. So whatever you've achieved, shout about it! Inspire others to put *their* best foot forward and push for change themselves. Pat yourself on the back for doing something to make society a better place! YOU DID IT.

DELAYS

Take the word 'failure' out of your lexicon unless it has actually happened. If you hear yourself saying it, correct yourself. Out loud. If you feel yourself thinking it, correct yourself. Out loud. Hearing yourself say it has no place in this game. In activism, there really isn't such a thing as failure, because any campaign, whatever size, goes some way towards progressing attitudes and society – no effort is wasted. However, stalling and delays can inevitably happen.

It's easy to recognise a delay as a failure or 'the end'. It doesn't have to be. It's not over until you say it is.

When my Private Members' Bill to make upskirting a sexual offence was blocked by Christopher Chope in June 2018, I could have taken that as the end of the road. I could have left the room and thought that was it. If he did it once, surely he'll stand his ground and do it again? He's not going to change his mind, otherwise his objection in the first place was moot . . . I thought. But that's the point about activism. That's why I love it so much.

No one can tell you when your job is done. You made that job. You created it. And no one but you gets to decide when that job is finished. It's up to you to pull yourself back up again, however hard it feels, and carry on. But remember, that doesn't have to happen straight away. Prioritising yourself, your mental health and your physical health is critical and if you need to lie in bed for two days, rest, watch movies and eat eighteen bowls of pasta before you can get back to work, do it. This timeline is yours, no one else's.

'FAILURE'

Activism is often about pushing for change unconventionally and creating new processes as well as using the original ones. It's about trying to do something that not many people try to do. Activists are already in the minority and therefore you are up against many barriers, complex systems and outside forces. To prevail in a system that doesn't want you to do things differently is hard, and there may be instances when you literally don't achieve the thing you set out to achieve. Whilst feminism has moved beyond the second-wave writings of Catharine MacKinnon and Andrea Dworkin, their efforts to change pornography laws in the 1980s mirror problems that activists can face today: they had to set out a legislative approach based on human rights rather than obscenity in order to call for pornography to be outlawed and to allow damage suits against pornographers, working around the terms of the law. Although their specific efforts were largely unsuccessful, their work led to so much progress in this field. What I'm saying is, not achieving your specific objective is tough, but you have still left a legacy, and paved the way for others. Remember, though, that if you are struggling with not having achieved your goal, taking time for yourself is key. Surround yourself with those who love you, seek out and digest the positives that have come from your work, and make a conscious effort to engage with those who support it. Then, remember to carry on your work in some way. Whether that's writing, speaking, hosting dinners, creating a platform or anything else, your efforts are too important not to continue just because this one thing didn't work out as you'd hoped. You've got this.

MAKING SURE YOUR WORK LIVES ON

In my mind there's one thing that is just as good as leading by example: inspiring people and passing on information. Every experience you've taken on during campaigning can be a lesson or inspirational for other people, so make sure your work lives on somehow and continues to add value to society after the main campaign is finished. This book is an example of how I want my work to live on, but yours might be workshops, speaking gigs, starter packs, a website, a blog, an annual magazine or event, or – *quelle surprise* – another campaign! The possibilities are endless. But I can guarantee that when you've done this once, you won't want to stop. Action is addictive, because it is the real antidote to fear and worry. Making the world a better place is too good a feeling to let go, and if you can inspire others to embark on that work too, then do it. We need more of you.

AFTERWORD

A letter to activists in training

You picked up this book for a reason; you want to make things better for people. It's going to be hard at times, and it may push you to your limits, but what better to be challenged by than the pursuit of making the world a better place? Don't lose yourself in the madness – be proud of your idiosyncrasies. Be human throughout it all and show it. We need more people who understand us to look up to. Don't apologise for caring too much about the world, and don't make excuses for feeling so deeply. Know when you're right and admit when you're wrong. Realise you won't get things perfect the first time, and neither should you – you only become better by failing. Treat yourself as the top priority while you fight for what you believe in, because you can't make things better for others if you don't have standards for yourself. Keep learning, and throw yourself into research if you find you've stopped. Our work is never done as activists; we are always learning and growing. Ground your work in compassion for everyone. You can be opinionated, you can be bold and you can push your agenda, but if it doesn't come from a place of inclusion and tolerance, it isn't right and it will result, whether inadvertently or not, in segregating people in some way. You don't need to be perfect – we are done with asking everything of those we look up to, and instead need a more diverse set of individuals doing great things. You don't need to be infallible. Take yourself out of the fight – this is not just about you but all of us. Stop apologising. Fake your confidence but not your facts. Ask for help whenever you need it and know your limits. Be clever, be strategic and be bold. Be proud of yourself for even trying.

I'll see you out there making the world a better place. I'll see you out there being the change.

Gina xx

FURTHER RESOURCES

BOOKS

We Should All Be Feminists by Chimamanda Ngozi Adichie
Why I'm No Longer Talking to White People About Race by Reni
   Eddo-Lodge
White Fragility by Robin DiAngelo
Sapiens by Yuval Noah Harari
The Will to Change by bell hooks
Outrageous Acts and Everyday Rebellions by Gloria Steinem
Fight Like A Girl by Clementine Ford
Invisible Women by Caroline Criado-Perez
The Multi-Hyphen Method by Emma Gannon
Little Black Book by Otegha Uwagba
The Uninhabitable Earth by David Wallace-Wells

PODCASTS

About Race with Reni Eddo-Lodge
Getting Curious with Jonathan Van Ness
Reasons to be Cheerful with Ed Miliband and Geoff Lloyd
Unsubscribe with Jada Sezer and Louise Troen
The High Low with Pandora Sykes and Dolly Alderton
Today in Focus (the *Guardian*)

ACKNOWLEDGEMENTS

Abigail Bergstrom and Megan Staunton at Gleam Titles for guiding me through this mad time and making everything easier for me.

Hannah Boursnell for being a dreamy editor and totally getting, from the beginning, why this book needed to be written.

Aimee Kitson, Stephanie Melrose and Sophia Schoepfer for being a kick-ass team and putting a fire hose behind *Be the Change*.

Bekki Guyatt for the awesome cover.

Aja Barber for being a brilliant educator, getting stuck in with this book and teaching me so much. You can find Aja at @etoilee8 on Twitter, or @ajabarber on Instagram.

INDEX

SHARE YOUR ACTIVISM JOURNEY ON SOCIAL MEDIA USING THE HASHTAG #BETHECHANGE

INSTAGRAM
@ginamartinuk

TWITTER
@ginamartin_uk